Scott Martin

NEW DIRECTIONS IN TAROT

Decoding the Tarot Illustrations of
PAMELA COLMAN SMITH

REDFeather™
MIND | BODY | SPIRIT
4880 Lower Valley Road, Atglen, PA 19310

Cover and interior designed by BMac
Type set in Minion Pro/New Frank
Cover and inside illustration of Pamela Colman Smith
by James Boyle (jamesboyle.com)
Rights to reproduce the poster image of "Pamela Colman Smith-Life and Work," courtesy of Pratt Institute Libraries, Brooklyn, New York

ISBN: 978-0-7643-6630-7
Printed in China

Published by REDFeather Mind, Body, Spirit
An imprint of Schiffer Publishing, Ltd.
4880 Lower Valley Road
Atglen, PA 19310
Phone: (610) 593-1777; Fax: (610) 593-2002
Email: Info@redfeathermbs.com
Web: www.redfeathermbs.com

For our complete selection of fine books on this and related subjects, please visit our website at www.schifferbooks.com. You may also write for a free catalog.

REDFeather Mind, Body, Spirit's titles are available at special discounts for bulk purchases for sales promotions or premiums. Special editions, including personalized covers, corporate imprints, and excerpts, can be created in large quantities for special needs. For more information, contact the publisher.

We are always looking for people to write books on new and related subjects. If you have an idea for a book, please contact us at proposals@schifferbooks.com.

To Pamela Colman Smith
Who Inspired Us All

And in loving memory
of my dear friend and mentor,
Rachel Pollack

ACKNOWLEDGMENTS

PAMELA COLMAN SMITH, THE UNTOLD STORY, by Stuart R. Kaplan with Mary K. Greer, Elizabeth Foley O'Connor, and Melinda Boyd Parsons, sparked my interest in this fascinating woman, whom I had known primarily as the last name on the Rider-Waite-Smith Tarot deck.

A special thanks to Mary K. Greer and Robert M. Place for their encouragement and for their very helpful guidance and suggestions.

I sent an early version of my manuscript to Mary K. Greer, who said I could quote her:

> OMG, I'm only up to page 30 and absolutely loving it!!! Of course, I have some suggestions—partly because this is such an eye-opener and vastly helpful for interpretation!" . . . "Wow! It really makes the reading come alive! . . . What fun. This is brilliant!

Proofreaders and friends with keen intellects, objectivity, and attentiveness to details are invaluable to an author. I value my friends, those initial "editors": Marie Pauwels, Paul Quinn, Philip Banyon, and Frank Lopardo; in all of those respects, I thank you all!

Once again, I would like to thank the staff at Remsen Graphics, 52 Court Street, Brooklyn, NY 11201, Remsen165aol.com, for their excellent printing and binding of the early copies of the manuscripts. They are the consummate professionals. Their friendly staff, led by Michael and Piero Galluzzo, makes doing business with them a real pleasure.

And to all my wonderful teachers along the way: Wald and Ruth Amberstone, Ellen Goldberg, Elinor Greenberg, Mary K. Greer, Robert M. Place, and Rachel Pollack. And as always to my friend Sasha Graham, and one-time fellow student in the Tarot School in NYC, who wanted to be the first person to pay me for a reading and then later insisted that I write a book. This is my third. Thank you, Sasha!

CONTENTS

FOREWORD

BY MARY K. GREER

I am so excited to be introducing you to Scott Martin's book on using theatrical conventions for interpreting Tarot cards and spreads with the Rider-Waite-Smith Tarot deck. As Martin explains, the artist was Pamela Colman Smith (known as Pixie, a name given to her by English actress Ellen Terry), who spent much of her early life involved in the theater, from miniature stage productions to set and costume design to her own costumed storytelling performances. She not only worked in one of the major theater companies of the period, Henry Irving's Lyceum Theatre Company, but also tried to sell several art projects to publishers featuring the plays of Shakespeare, which she knew well. Scott Martin's professional life and experience in every aspect of theater makes Smith's own knowledge of stagecraft apparent and also useful to us as readers of the cards.

When Martin first came to me with a draft of this book, I found it both tremendous fun and brilliantly eye-opening to see how helpful these standard conventions are to card interpretations, especially for the Minor Arcana, over which Smith had predominant design control. The systems presented here are logical and simple to learn, and once you do, they can work for you without your having to think much about them. Martin's explanations of theatrical staging took me immediately back to my own introduction to Tarot.

When I first discovered Tarot in 1967, I was minoring in theater in college, taking classes, and being involved in play production in every capacity, so the conventions presented in this book were well known to me. I remembered discussions on the importance of setting the scene at the moment the curtain rises, and concerns over "upstaging" as well as the dynamics of blocking and entrances and exits.

Thinking back in time, I'm now even more aware of how my acting classes influenced my initial approach to Tarot. The realization came to me when reading Martin's manuscript that the exercises and "games" in my acting classes and my experiences with late '60s encounter groups and consciousness raising were nearly identical.

How do we know that theatrical conventions informed Smith's illustrations? Martin mentions some of her use of theatrical portraits and scenes as a basis for several cards in the Minor Arcana. Another factor is a selection of fourteen or more cards that have come to be called "stage cards" because the lower foreground consists of a flat platform, looking like a nearly bare stage, and is separated from a scenic backdrop by a double horizontal line.

An article by Pamela Colman Smith titled "Appropriate Stage Decoration" appeared in the *New Age* magazine (vol. 7, no. 5 [June 2, 1910]: 7–9) shortly after the deck was published. It perfectly supports Scott Martin's approach in this book.

Smith begins:

> About us is the glowing beauty of the world, with its leaves and flowers, rags, gold, and purple. Kings on thrones of iron, beggars on beds of clay, laughing, weeping, dreaming. This pageant of life moves before us, intensified, in the theatre. [It is] an exaggeration of life, a march of characters before our eyes.

In a Tarot reading, we have a progression of scenes whose figures are comparable to ourselves and to those with whom we are involved. It is this intensification of a personal issue in a person's life that helps them recognize a repeating theme and, if desired, begin to change it.

Smith disparages too-realistic scenery, claiming,

> Those in power have not remembered that illusion is the aim of the theatre. It is a great game of pretense . . . a remnant of that imaginative life we relive in beholding a play set forth before our eyes. If the illusion is good, we follow it more easily. Realism is not Art. It is the essence that is necessary to give a semblance of the real thing. . . . .Everything must be exaggerated in order that it may be visible across the footlights.

A fantasy fairy tale, as in Pamela's faux medieval Minor Arcana, can allow us to imaginatively inhabit it and, in doing so, come to see a dramatic story playing out in our own lives.

Why should this theatrical approach be important to you? The trick is to first see what scene is being played out on the stage, and then to see it as a metaphor for one's own life. When a querent first describes the story, they can then repeat what they've said as "I statements" (owning everything as an aspect of self). The theatrical scene thus reveals what is going on with and in that person. Major clues to the stories the cards tell can be found in the staging or blocking of the scenes—the keys to which are revealed in this book.

I strongly recommend doing the exercises! Scott Martin's techniques will make the Rider-Waite-Smith Tarot come alive in new and exciting ways, with the added benefit of your being able to watch a play with a deeper understanding of what is going on. I guarantee that using even one, much less all, of the insights included here will add immeasurably to your experience with the deck. I'm so pleased to introduce a brilliant new approach to reading the most-iconic Tarot cards of the twentieth and twenty-first centuries.

—Mary K. Greer
December 2021

PAMELA COLMAN SMITH
AND HER MINORS: THE WAITE-SMITH TAROT
AS "MINIATURE THEATRE"

Pamela Colman Smith has been a rather elusive figure until recently. For all that was known about her, much remained a matter of supposition. But we do know that she was an artist in the theater, a creative genius, a mystic, and a clairvoyant in her own right. However, she will be best remembered as the artist who in 1909 designed pictures on seventy-eight Tarot cards that became known as the Rider-Waite-Smith Tarot deck; this deck became the most famous and iconic Tarot deck of its time and is still the most widely used today.

In the mid-1890s, Smith attended Pratt Institute of Art in Clinton Hill, Brooklyn, New York, just 2 miles from my home in Brooklyn Heights. As a matter of fact, I visited a collection of hers there in 2019 (see appendix III).

She inherited her love for the theater quite naturally. Her mother, Corinne Colman, performed in Brooklyn Heights as an amateur actress and was admired for her fine acting prowess (Kaplan et al. 2018).

And so, at an early age, she was to the manor born.

Arthur Edward Waite, cocreator of the Waite-Smith deck, and Pamela Colman Smith became acquainted through their association in the Golden Dawn, a secret society devoted to the study and practice of the occult, metaphysics, and paranormal activities. There are books that cover what is known of her history there. But my curiosity led me in another direction, one of imagining to what extent might her theater background have informed her illustrations.

It is a daunting challenge to pinpoint where one influence ends and the next begins. How does one separate the warp from the weave? In the *Craftsmen Magazine*, Ms. Smith wrote an article in 1906 titled "Should the Art Student Think?" (see appendix IV). In it, she said that

the stage is a great school . . . to the illustrator. . . . First watch the simple forms of joy, of fear, of sorrow; look at the position taken of the whole body, then the face. . . . After you have learned to tell a simple story, put in more details, the face, and indicate the dress. . . . The stage has taught me almost all I know of clothes, of actions, and of pictorial gestures. (Kaplan et al. 2018)

Much of what she espouses in this article supports my thesis by assuring us that much of her inspiration as an artist came from her experience in the theater, her knowledge of theatrical staging, and the actor's instrument.

It is no wonder then that this Tarot project came so innately to Smith, who spent most of her life in the theater. As a child she participated in amateur theatrics. As an adult she appeared in minor roles in productions that starred Ellen Terry, one of the renowned English actresses who performed extensively throughout Great Britain and North America in the late nineteenth and early twentieth centuries. She may be best remembered for her role as Lady Macbeth. We know that Smith was well acquainted with this famous actress of the time, as well as her daughter, Edy Craig, and son, Edward Gordon Craig. Ellen Terry is said to be immortalized by Smith in her Queen of Wands, though *Pamela Colman Smith, the Untold Story* suggests that the Nine of Pentacles is the more obvious re-creation as the older, wealthy Ellen Terry.

Katz and Goodwin also believe that there are other cards inspired by characters from plays with which she was surely familiar: the Nine of Cups—Falstaff in *Henry IV*, parts I and II; the Nine of Pentacles—Rosalind from *As You Like It*; and the Two of Cups—Romeo and Juliet in a play of the same name. The three figures in the Three of Cups purportedly come from Smith's personal life: Smith herself, accompanied by Ellen Terry and Terry's daughter, Edy Craig (Katz and Goodwin 2015).

Ellen Terry's son, Edward Gordon Craig, was an accomplished scenic designer, who no doubt further influenced Smith's interest in set design. She went on to work as a scenic and costume designer in several London theaters, including the Lyceum Theatre in London's West End, an unusual profession for a woman at that time (Katz and Goodwin 2015). Smith was breaking through "the glass ceiling" before the term was ever coined.

In *Pamela Colman Smith, the Untold Story*, we learn that Smith famously designed her own "Miniature Theatre." The theater house was approximately 18 inches square. Her one-dimensional characters were on a scale not much larger than the figures we see on her Tarot cards. So, moving from her Miniature Theatre to designing Tarot cards with figures, costumes, and scenery must have been a rather seamless transition. We can easily imagine that as she drew each card, she was envisioning the characters performing and moving about in the scaled-down world of her imagination. She would be, in effect, "dressing the stage." In production terms, this refers to decorating the stage with furniture, props, wall hangings, and the like. But it also includes actors. If, in rehearsal, the director spoke to the actors and said, "Dress the stage," he was relying on their "stage sense" to adjust their locations on the stage to create a more balanced stage picture.

A. E. Waite visualized the deck and communicated the Major Arcana images in some detail to Smith; he was clearly influenced by the French Marseille deck for his vision of those, but he left the Minors largely for Smith to ruminate and cast her theatrically imaginative spell (Kaplan et al. 2018).

It is said that Waite wanted all seventy-eight cards illustrated, and he referred Smith to the fifteenth-century Italian *Sola Busca* Tarot deck for inspiration. It was the first deck that illustrated all seventy-eight cards. Waite was very specific regarding his vision for the Majors. However, the Minors, left essentially to Smith's imaginings, are arguably the most remarkable achievement of the Waite-Smith deck.

Prior to Smith incorporating characters in her Minors, Ace through Ten were referred to as "pips," as in the Marseille deck, for example. The cards were grouped by suits—Wands, Swords, Cups, and Pentacles—and were identified by the number of the symbols of their suit. For instance, the Four of Swords displayed a drawing of four swords and so forth. The court cards, however, were traditionally illustrated with characters.

Smith's Three of Swords and Queen of Cups particularly are reminiscent of the fifteenth-century Italian *Sola Busca*, and several other cards that show figures who look overly burdened, carrying the symbols of their suit; those cards are rather like the Ten of Wands in Smith's Minors. One may make the case that all the court cards of the *Sola Busca* also influenced Smith when she designed her courts. But the Minors in the Waite-Smith deck are solely products of her creation, though her inspirations may have come in part from the *Sola Busca* Tarot deck, Etteilla, the Golden Dawn, and her observations of paintings in the British Museum. However, while those influences are not to be discounted, her intuitive nature and her life in the theater move front and center when it comes to prioritizing their relative worth as motivators to her visions.

Once I delved into the history of this deck, I began to look at the Majors and Minors quite differently. The Majors looked rather staid, as though they were posing for their portrait, while the Minors were reminiscent of a still frame from a moving picture; they breathed life, movement, and mood. The pictures engaged the viewer in imagining what was going to happen in the next frame as the plot unfolded.

Wald Amberstone, cofounder of the Tarot School and the Readers' Studio along with his wife, Ruth Amberstone, makes an interesting distinction between the Majors and the Minors. He says, "Generally speaking, the Minor Arcana describes what there is to see, while the Major Arcana describes the inner world of the seer."

Smith's life in the theater particularly resonated with me. There was much there to which I could relate. I was also introduced to the theater at a young age and spent my professional life there. I have worked professionally as an actor and director as well as in community and educational theater. I have designed costumes and sets. I taught theater arts for forty years, both on the high school and college levels. As a result, I am well acquainted with stage movement—how characters move, why they move, where they move, their gait, their posture, their stance, their gestures, and their facial expressions.

It is from this background that I propose to explore how I think Smith's theatrical knowledge and experience came into play when she drew these cards. Although, with few exceptions, I will not include the symbolism of the Golden Dawn, I know that symbolism and titles play a major role in understanding the meanings of each card, so I will include all of the esoteric titles as a matter of interest.

CHAPTER ONE

PAMELA COLMAN SMITH
AS STORYTELLER—"A PERFECT MATCH"

Coming to Tarot from her work in the theater was a natural for Pamela Colman Smith. She was well versed in the history of theater, parts of a play, structure of a plot, nature of conflict, and various design elements of scenery and costume design. All that background and experience must have been at play on some level in all the cards that she designed.

Undoubtedly, she would have been familiar with the elements of storytelling in theater as described in Aristotle's *The Poetics*, 335 CE, the earliest surviving work on dramatic theory. This Golden Age of Greece gave us the building blocks of our civilization: great monuments, art, philosophy, architecture, and literature, and, in this discussion, Aristotle's Six Elements of a Play: Plot, Character, Thought, Dialogue, Music, and Spectacle.

However, the roots of storytelling are as old as time. In its most primitive form, cave men wore animal skins, while others carried crude weapons and "dramatized" the hunt as they danced around the campfire. This ritual was meant to bring luck to the hunt and thus provide food for the clan.

Throughout time, humankind has turned to storytelling as a way of chronicling their history, first from mouth to mouth, then through pictures carved in stone, and later in written language. Paul Foster Case, an early member of the Golden Dawn and founder of B.O.T.A. (Builders of the Adytum), tells us that "Tarot is a book, disguised as a deck of cards." This book encapsulates man's journey from emanation of spirit to manifestation in the mundane world.

Both the Tarot Minors and theater tell stories through characters to reflect themselves, the world around them, and their interactions with others. They contain themes of love, passion, ambition, mental challenges, and extraordinary circumstances that interrupt what otherwise could have been a rather ordinary life. They both are dressed in the technical elements of the theater: sets, costumes, props, and lighting.

Taking one element at a time, note how it manifests in Smith's Tarot deck.

PLOT

Tarot is a master at storytelling. Let's take the Nine of Wands, for example:

One need not be an expert in reading Tarot cards to spin a very interesting tale about the character in this card. It is rich with prompts for discussion: the bandage on the man's head, the expression on his face, the tight grip he holds on his wand, the direction of his glance, and so on. The details of the story will take shape in the context of the querent's question.

But before developing a scene, let's define a few more elements of drama that Smith integrated into her illustrations: one element all plays have in common in order to be dramatically interesting is conflict.

CONFLICT

Examples of Dramatic Conflict Illustrated in the Tarot. ***Please note*** that throughout this book you'll find exercises to help build your understanding of the concepts. You may want to jot your answers in a journal or notebook to reflect on later.

Exercise

Select three other cards for each type of the five types of conflicts shown on the next page, using the full deck if you wish.

Types of Plays

1. A comedy is a realistic play with three-dimensional characters and is generally humorous. The characters and situations are rather ordinary. We see these people every day in our comings and goings. The emphasis is on character. We care about the character. That is, we want to know what's going to happen to our main character (hero/heroine) throughout the play. They generally overcome the conflict, using their wit and intelligence (the Four of Wands, the Three of Cups). ***Add one more.***

2. A serious drama, other than the fact that it is obviously serious, contains most of the other elements of a comedy. We are most interested in the main character and what

MAN VS. MAN   MAN VS. HIMSELF

MAN VS. SOCIETY   MAN VS. NATURE

MAN VS. SUPERNATURAL

happens to him; he usually overcomes the conflict. The main character is well developed and three-dimensional, but of no heroic stature (the Five of Pentacles, the Nine of Swords). *Add one more.*

3. A tragedy is a serious drama about an extraordinary, three-dimensional character whom we greatly admire and look up to; he is a "tragic hero." The emphasis is on character. He is overcome by the conflict by way of a "tragic flaw," usually seen in the form of hubris, fate, mental weakness, or maladjustment (the Ten of Swords, the Five of Cups). *Add one more.*

4. A melodrama. In the types above, the emphasis is on a character. Here, in the final two, the emphasis shifts to situation. We're not as concerned about what's going to happen to our rather one-dimensional, stereotypical main character, but rather, what's going to happen next in the plot. It is plot, not character, driven. It is characterized by chills, spills, scares, danger, and fast action, while still following a rather predictable plot to a certain point; at the climax, something extraordinarily unexpected occurs, which changes the expected outcome and saves the day for our main character from a very undesirable fate (the Tower, the Devil). *Add one more.*

5. A farce is a ridiculously silly play, written for sheer laughs—no life lessons here. The characters are one-dimensional, just as in melodrama: no depth. It is often called "slapstick comedy." The main character always wins using his wit, buffoonery, and horseplay, which typically include crude characterization and ludicrously improbable situations (the Nine of Cups, the Two of Pentacles). *Add one more.*

Exercise

PLOT OUTLINE
Smith had an uncanny talent for "writing a two-act play" all within the sight lines of one Tarot card. Try it for yourself. Choose a card that is ripe with prompts that suggest an interesting and perhaps complex story. It doesn't have to have anything to do with what you already know of the card. In fact, it would challenge your imagination even more by telling a story that is plausible yet quite different from what usually may come to mind. Write a brief plot outline based on the card you choose.

Character

While plot is the story, characters are the storytellers. Let's take another look at the Nine of Wands. Is there any doubt who this man is in your mind when you look again at his picture?

I, who am not an artist by any stretch of the imagination, had to trace paper doll cutouts in my costume design class in graduate school to arrive at a silhouette of a human form onto the costume plate. However, if the character silhouette required more than that, I had to call on my friend and artist Bobby Rodriguez to draw the shape for me. A memorable example was the rather rotund Julius Caesar in the children's theater production of Androcles in the Lion. Smith did not share my artistic challenges. She clearly wanted to make a statement about this character below in the Nine of Cups by, in part, his body type and the way he sits (legs spread with arms folded across his chest), with a rather contented, self-satisfied expression on his face.

Exercise

Select a character illustrated on one of the other Tarot cards. Choose one with very distinct features in terms of body type, posture, gait, facial expression, angle of pose, SR, SL, FF (abbreviations for stage right, stage left, and full front), overall physical demeanor or attitude, and if the character seems to have a destination in mind. If the character is in a standing or sitting position, does he/she seem to be there briefly or for an extended period of time? Again, apart from what you already know about this card, create another character that would be fitting to your description. The focus in these exercises is always on the physical lives of the characters. Write a brief character sketch of your new version of this card. It could even be the same character, but a different aspect of his personality or character (or both) that you had not considered before.

If no other card comes to mind right away, you may wish to write a character sketch on the figure in the Nine of Cups. The following are a few examples of items to include in your personality inventory:

- age
- physical appearance
- dress
- a typical physical mannerism
- posture
- family background
- education
- place in the community
- occupation, ambitions
- really good at [fill in the blank]
- temperament
- overarching attitude
- major obstacles
- self-image
- interaction with others

Include as many others as you wish.

Name of your card:_____

Character Sketch

THOUGHT

In the modern theater, thought translates as Theme. In the Majors, we find our themes in the archetypes; in the Minors we find them in the names of the suits: Wands, Swords, Cups, and Pentacles and their accompanying signs of Fire, Air, Water, and Earth.

The dramatic question is related to the central thematic idea on which the play is based. It is the question that most begs to be answered by the play's conclusion. For example, Will Romeo and Juliet live happily ever after? Will Hamlet avenge the murder of his father? Can Oscar and Felix, two straight, divorced men, live compatibly as roommates? And yes, even in fairy tales, will Cinderella marry the Prince?

Tarot cards also pose dramatic questions, arguably more than one, but here is a list of dramatic questions that each of the Tarot Minors may express. All Tarot cards are active and are in process; they burst with energy, so the dramatic question for the card in a spread will change, depending on the nature of the question and the other cards that surround it. The questions posed here are general and could be adapted for any number of subjects. The dramatic question is inextricably linked with the characters, intention/objective—what the character ultimately wants by the end of the play. One example has been provided for each of the cards that follow.

In your journal or notebook, write another dramatic question of your own for each of the cards that follow.

Exercise

WANDS

ACE Will inspiration create new opportunities?

TWO Will new discoveries reinvigorate him?

THREE Will his investments produce worthwhile dividends?

FOUR Will they be brought together in joyful celebration with the community?

FIVE Will this horseplay devolve into serious combat?

SIX Will the victor remain victorious?

SEVEN Will he persevere and maintain control in a difficult and challenging environment?

EIGHT Will quick and speedy action save the day?

NINE Will past experience prepare him for real or imagined foes?

TEN Will he have the strength and endurance to sustain his heavy burdens?

PAGE Will he make good use of his youthful exuberance?

KNIGHT Will his passion be diminished by his impulsiveness?

QUEEN Will her courage and confidence persevere and inspire others?

KING Will his natural-born leadership serve him and others well?

SWORDS

ACE Will mental clarity bring about a breakthrough?

TWO Will she make the best decision after carefully weighing her options?

THREE Will he/she find a way to release the pain from an emotional hurt and grow from it?

FOUR Will the time-out be restorative and enable him to resume his work with renewed devotion?

FIVE Will he settle for nothing less than winning at all costs?

SIX Will leaving a troublesome situation leave the trouble behind them?

SEVEN Will his tactics be successful in regaining what he thinks is rightfully his?

EIGHT Will she be able to get out of her own way and move forward?

NINE Will she be able to separate her fears and anxieties from reality and seek help to heal?

TEN Will this painful ending pave the way for a better beginning?

PAGE Will his curiosity and inquisitive mind open up new avenues of communication?

KNIGHT Will his ambition and quick thinking, born out of the thirst for action, lead him to success?

QUEEN Will she be able to modify her sharp rhetoric so that her valuable advice will be heard and accepted?

KING Will he employ his power, authority, and mental clarity to support others in seeing the truth?

CUPS

ACE Will the seeds of love begin to grow in your heart?

TWO Will a new and compatible partnership evolve and develop?

THREE Will a new group of friends bring joy and celebration to a life that has grown stale and boring?

FOUR Will he see a golden opportunity offered him, or will he ignore it?

FIVE Will he able to pick up the pieces and move on after he has processed the loss?

SIX Will reliving childhood memories bring joy or reminders of times best forgotten?

SEVEN Will he be able to make the best decision when he is overwhelmed by an abundance of choices?

EIGHT Is what he's leaving going to be worth the risk he's taking?

NINE Will physical and worldly indulgences satisfy his inner longings?

TEN Will family love be the catalyst that sustains them through life's unpredictable twists and turns?

PAGE Will his imagination and creative curiosity lead him to a fulfilling career in the arts?

KNIGHT Will his romantic imaginings and flights of fancy prevent his being a committed partner?

QUEEN Will her compassionate caring enable her to remain emotionally stable?

KING Will his compassion for others and deeply felt emotions enhance or hinder his ability to be an effective leader?

PENTACLES

ACE Will a new career or financial opportunity present itself?

TWO Can a multitasker still manage all his responsibilities effectively?

THREE Will teamwork empower the contributions of each individual member?

FOUR Will managing his financial resources bode well for his future security and for those in his charge?

FIVE Will their perseverance see them through these difficult and challenging times?

SIX Will he manage the boundaries between giving and receiving so that he can manage the two compatibly?

SEVEN Will he maintain his long-term vision when his immediate rewards may be less than expected?

EIGHT Will his devoted commitment to his apprenticeship lead to mastery?

NINE Will her self-sufficient lifestyle and financial independence provide all she needs for emotional happiness?

TEN Will family finances be shared fairly and equitably to avoid the dark side of wealth?

PAGE Is he beginning a career that will lead to the development of a skill and financial success?

KNIGHT Will hard work, conservative thinking, and routine be enough to sustain a rewarding life and career?

QUEEN Will her need to nurture and protect find a new outlet during the "empty nest" syndrome?

KING Will a potential obsession with wealth and status outweigh his ability to lead effectively?

THOUGHT (THEME)

When we look at the Two of Cups, the theme of Love and Harmony naturally comes to mind.

Exercise

Turn over your deck one card at a time until a card strikes you that communicates a theme or the main idea. We just noticed that the Two of Cups speak to the theme of Love. Choose another card that unmistakably says "theme" to you. What is that theme, and how is it manifest in the visual aspects of the card? Justify your choice in a brief, written paragraph in your journal or notebook.

Name of Card _____

Theme _____

Written Paragraph (**record this in your journal or notebook**)

DIALOGUE

Dialogue is the spoken word between or among characters in a play. When one character is the only one speaking, it is a monologue, a soliloquy or an aside, or a "throw away." Here we must use our imagination to fill in the dialogue, since there are no written words on the Waite-Smith cards, save for their names. However, combined with what we know of the cards and the illustrated given circumstances, we can easily write the script. The Golden Dawn's esoteric titles could certainly prompt one into imagining dialogue as well. As I studied all the Minors, I noticed that Swords seemed to be the "quietest" of the suits, though the symbol of its suit is powerful. Perhaps they represent the "strong, silent type." After all, Swords are the suit of the mind. There are three characters in the Six of Swords, but the tone feels somber and heavy, so it would be difficult to imagine that there is much to be spoken aloud.

When I write about Tarot, I am often drawn to Kahlil Gibran's The Prophet, and this is certainly true as I reflect of the Six of Swords: "For without words, in friendship, all thoughts, all desires, all expectations are born and shared, with joy that is unacclaimed."

Exercise

DIALOGUE

Choose a Tarot card with more than one character. You may be drawn to one of those shown on the next page. Set the scene for yourself:

Who are they?
What is their relationship?
What do they want from each other? (Objective)

Rather than just casual conversation, make the scene important to the development to the plot; "Raise the stakes" so that a great deal can be gained or lost as a result of the outcome. Make it a defining moment . . . no turning back now. Write ten lines of dialogue that will bring this scene to its climax. Keep in the mind the characters' physical interactions with each other, their facial expressions, how they face and approach each other, and why, where, and how they move. Use the space below or write in your journal or notebook.

_____

_____

_____

_____

MUSIC

There is a debate among theater historians about what Aristotle meant by "Music" in The Poetics, and it will not be settled here. Nonetheless, many believe that there were musicians playing instruments in an area in front of the amphitheater known as the "orchestra," a term still in use today to delineate the area in which the musicians are located. We also know that there was a chorus in ancient Greek plays, played by one

Cards to consider for the DIALOGUE Exercise.

player who was apart from the action but observed and commented on what was taking place onstage. These "comments" could have evolved into a kind of songlike chanting. The chorus would often leave the stage to change into the costume of another character.

Others believe that Aristotle was referring to the melody of the spoken Greek language, which has a pleasingly lyrical quality when spoken beautifully.

I think of music in the cards in yet another away. A Tarot "orchestra" might also be compared to musical instruments by the way the card "sounds." If we think of the personality of the happy-go-lucky young fellow in the Two of Pentacles, we may be reminded of a C flute or a piccolo, while if we "listen" to the Five of Cups, we may "hear" the haunting and forlorn sounds of an oboe.

Exercise

Go through your deck again and choose two cards in which you think you can "hear" music. Try to find contrasting cards that convey quite different thoughts or moods. The music may not be coming from a musical instrument; it could be the sound of wind blowing through the trees in a storm, a babbling brook, the banging of pots or pans, or perhaps the cacophony of human voices—yelling, chanting, cheering, or singing. Describe in a written paragraph the "music" you hear when you meditate on these two cards, and describe how Smith's illustrations brought those sounds of "music" to mind.

1. Card_____ Source of Music_____

2. Card_____ Source of Music_____

SPECTACLE

Spectacle is all that we see or that enables us to see onstage and, by extension, all that we hear, with the exception of the orchestra. As a director and set and costume designer, Pamela Colman Smith was definitely quite familiar with all these elements: sets, costumes, props, makeup, lighting, and sound.

    Shown above are examples of four cards in which I think sets and costumes take center stage.

    The design elements of a play have just as much a role in storytelling as any other aspect of the play.

    No doubt, a story could be written with a beginning, middle, and ending, just by stepping inside any one of these four cards. Smith has provided all the cues.

Exercise

Select a card that is rich in design details: indoors or outdoors, bright or somber, spacious or crowded. If there is a character or characters pictured on the card, remove them from your mind for this exercise. Pretend the curtain opens on Act I, bare of characters. In terms of design elements, what type of play do you think this production has in store for you: comedy, tragedy, melodrama, serious drama, or farce? Write a paragraph in your journal or notebook describing the set and the kind of play for which it was designed. It is always important to remember the designers. They contribute a great deal in setting the mood, telling the story, and sustaining the audience's interest. Smith would have been involved in all these aspects of a production and would have applied much of what she knew when she designed the Waite-Smith Tarot deck.

Card_____

Type of Play_____

Defend your choice with five examples of what you see in the spectacle of the card.

    As Smith was drawing her cards, I could imagine her "starring" them in her beloved "Miniature Theatre" and visualizing a play around them.

Exercise

Choose one of the four cards shown on the opposite page or one of your own choosing, and build a plot outline. Use the chart below. The definitions for each part of a plot are listed on the next page. The card you choose could be at any point in the events of the story. Build around it.
    For example:

The Ten of Pentacles could be the Falling Action (events following the
    resolution of the conflict).
The Four of Wands, the Rising Action (events leading up to the climax).
The Nine of Swords, the Climax (the point of no return).
The Two of Wands, the Exposition (the backstory).

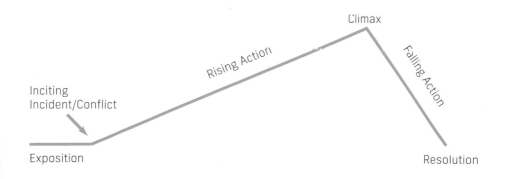

THE STRUCTURE OF A PLOT OF A PLAY

Exposition: Events before the action of the play begins (the backstory), sometimes referred to as the "backdrop."

1. Initial incident: Idea or action that introduces the central conflict (first event that takes place in real time; it hasn't occurred before). It moves the plot into its first forward direction.

2. Rising action: Main character acts to achieve goal or resolve problem (minor conflicts or complications introduced, also known as obstacles, building up to the climax).

3. Climax: Point of greatest interest—the point of no return.

4. Falling action: The events that occur as a result of what happens in the climax in order to overcome the obstacles (unraveling of the plot).

5. Dénouement: The strands of the plot are drawn together and matters are explained.

6. Conclusion: Final unraveling of plot; the story ends with the protagonist's success or failure.

Exercise

Select a play, movie, or TV drama with which you are familiar. Using the chart on the next page, write a plot outline on a separate piece of paper and include the following:

1. Identify a protagonist and an antagonist.

2. Each of them will have an objective that is very important and is in opposition to the other. "Raise the stakes" for each. A great deal will be won or lost on the basis of who overcomes the conflict.

3. Identify obstacles that will obstruct their path to victory for each of them.

4. Create tactics (maneuvers) for them in their attempt to overcome those obstacles.

5. End with a resolution: One wins; one loses.

DIRECTIONS
Briefly fill in your answers in the chart below:

EXPOSITION	CONFLICT	RISING ACTION

CLIMAX	FALLING ACTION	RESOLUTION

Exercise

Now apply what has been reviewed about the structure of a plot with examples from the Directions chart; relate them to one of the "stages of your own life" following, using the floor plan illustrated under chapter 2, "The Proscenium Stage," as a model. You may draw your own on a separate piece of paper.

CHAPTER TWO

THE PROSCENIUM STAGE

Most stages that Smith worked on would have been proscenium stages. This kind of stage gets its name from the large arch that separates the stage, located behind the arch, and the audience that sits in front of it (from the Greek, translated as the "arch" "in front of the scene": = proscenium).

Sometimes there is an *apron* on the stage, which is an extension of the stage and stretches beyond the proscenium. This too becomes an acting area. It brings the life of the play more intimately into the laps of the audience.

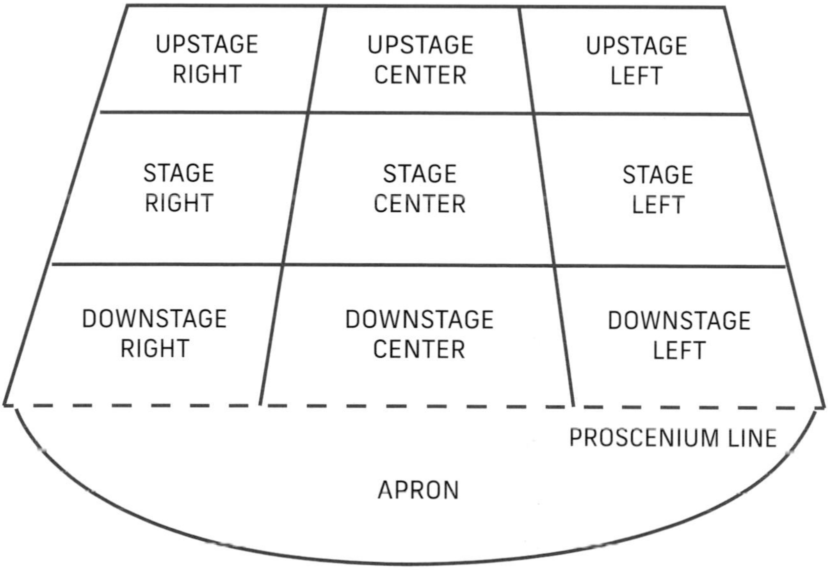

UPSTAGE RIGHT	UPSTAGE CENTER	UPSTAGE LEFT
STAGE RIGHT	STAGE CENTER	STAGE LEFT
DOWNSTAGE RIGHT	DOWNSTAGE CENTER	DOWNSTAGE LEFT

PROSCENIUM LINE

APRON

The stage is divided into nine acting areas as seen in the chart, known as "blocks." That is why, when a director is staging a play, the process is called "blocking"; that is, moving actors around the "blocks." In future references to these blocks, I will often refer to them by their abbreviations, such as DSR, for "downstage right" and so on (these blocks are not literally marked on the stage floor).

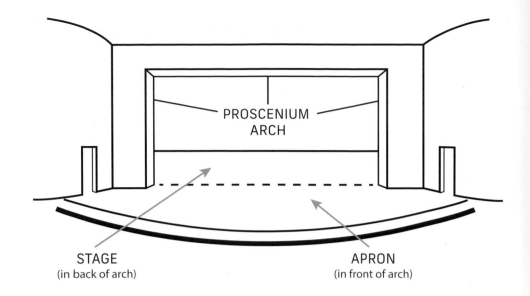

PROSCENIUM ARCH

STAGE
(in back of arch)

APRON
(in front of arch)

The area closest to the audience is called downstage (DS), and the area farthest away is upstage (US). One may say, why up and down when the stage is flat? In the medieval period, when plays were banned from the churches for taking on secular themes, actors, troubadours, and the like took to the streets. Many performed on wagons. When they were performing, one side of the wagon would be unhinged, lowered, and propped up on an angle with stakes. That and the interior of the wagon became the playing area of the "proscenium stage." So, literally, at one time, if a character moved toward the audience, he moved down the stage, and if he moved away from the audience, he moved up the stage. This was also called a "raked" stage. In most modern theaters, the stage is now flat and the audience section is raked, so that an audience member can see over the heads of those sitting in the rows in front of him. There are some productions that also use raked stages to suit the style or concept of the production. Think how more powerfully dramatic it is when an actor moves down toward the audience from a ramped stage. It is particularly effective in ballet and musical theater. The dancers' feet, when contacting the stage floor, can be seen and appreciated to a much-greater advantage.

Stage right and stage left are from the actor's perspective as he faces the audience. So, if an actor is moving from the left side of the stage to the right side of the stage, he is entering stage left (your right) and moving stage right (your left).

CHAPTER THREE

ACTING AREAS OF A STAGE
AND THEIR RELATIVE STRENGTHS

In general, downstage is stronger than upstage, and stage right is stronger than stage left.

High is stronger than low. High is achieved in a number of ways: standing is most obvious, and all body positions in between standing and lying down, each weaker than the one before.

Standing or sitting on elevated structures (e.g., thrones/throne-like platforms, steps, and other structures that elevate the figure) focuses attention, suggests power, establishes position, and conveys a sense of one in authority. Deus Ex Machina is usually thought of as an unexpected event that saves a seemingly hopeless situation and redirects the plot in a more desirable trajectory. However, in this instance, the deus ex machina provides the ultimate power position. In the ancient Greek and Roman theater, it was literally a scenic device flown in from above by a crane or some other such conveyance. Rather than a hand appearing through a cloud bearing a symbol of its suit, as we see in Smith's Aces, the hand may descend from above the stage, bearing a god or goddess who saves the day from an untenable predicament.

DSC, all things considered, is the strongest position onstage. However, a character rarely takes that position unless he is delivering a soliloquy or an aside or is having an intimate conversation with another character, presumably out of hearing range of the other characters onstage. In Smith's Minors, any character or object that is centered on the card is in a powerful position; the rest of the setting will determine the nature of that power.

DSR holds a close second to DSC. In Western society, if "feels" strong, given that we are oriented to read from left to right.

At lectures, quite often, particularly if the lecturer is using PowerPoint in her presentation, she often stands SR of the screen. This may be born out of tradition, intuition, or both.

From theater history we know that in the medieval mystery or miracle plays, which often depict heaven, Earth, and hell onstage simultaneously, we find that Heaven is SR, Earth is SC, and Hell is SL. There's a certain sense, then, that SR is "good," or "stronger, and SL is "bad," or "weaker."

I've directed four productions of *Fiddler on the Roof* and have seen even more. When Tevye, the milkman, speaks to God, he always addresses him from DSR. This is "tradition" and one of the strongest "blocks" of the stage.

Any area of a stage can be made stronger, because a particular set design shifts the point of focus. One way to do that is to elevate that area or to light an area in a way that draws the audience's attention to that location. A weaker area of a stage can also be made stronger by the director's concept and visualization, such as a group of actors focusing their attention of a particular character or part of the stage. The audience will be guided to look where the actors are focusing.

In the theater, entrances and exits of characters are important. An entrance of a character begins a new "beat"; an exit of a character also designates a "beat." Beats signal the beginning or ending of a "French scene," which is generally the resolution of a minor conflict. The scene is going to change because of the entrance or exit of a character or the resolution of a minor conflict, or both. An entrance is generally more important than an exit. It means our interest is heightened by the arrival of a new character; the scene, by necessity, is going to move in a new direction and assist in developing the plot. An entrance of a new character is usually stage right, and the exit of a character is usually stage left. With a "box set"—that is, a room with three walls visible and the fourth wall or downstage wall removed for viewing of the play by the audience—the entrance from the outside is traditionally SR (although we sometimes see it USC), and exits to other rooms in the structure are SL or USL.

Smith would have been aware of these blocking conventions and liberally used them when designing the cards, especially the Minor Arcana.

Waite had clearer visions about the Major Arcana, which he conveyed in much-greater detail to Smith. However, when it came to the renderings of the Minors, he gave her freer rein to follow her own theatrical instincts.

CHAPTER FOUR

ACTORS' POSITIONS ONSTAGE

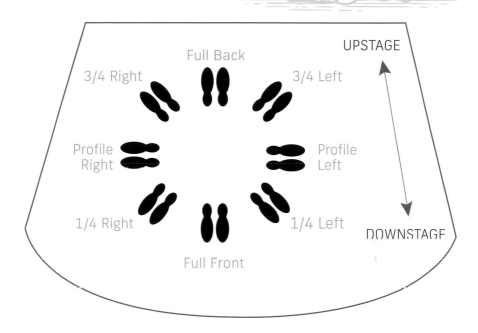

There are eight standing positions for a character onstage. These positions are the same for other body positions: as the actor faces the audience, these positions are full front, ¼ right (R), profile right, ¾ right, full back, ¾ left (L), profile left, and ¼ left.

If a character is DSC and facing the audience full front, he is likely "breaking the fourth wall" and addressing the audience or thinking out loud in a soliloquy. When a character is speaking directly to the audience, it is usually in a presentational style of play. That is, the play makes no pretense of depicting reality. It says in effect, "This is a play; we are actors, and we know there is an audience watching us; we can hear you breathing, *and your phones ringing*, and sometimes we are going to talk directly to you." A realistic play that asks the audience to accept the illusion of reality is referred to as a representational play. In that case, the actors would "observe the fourth wall"; that is, act as though the wall were actually there.

Full front (and full back, for that matter) is also the most vulnerable of all body positions, because they leave the entire body open to potential attack. Full front may also suggest ego, self-confidence—nothing to hide. What might you deduce about Smith's characters who are illustrated in this position?

When two characters are engaged in dialogue, they are traditionally standing in a ¼ R and ¼ L position to each other. This is called "sharing the scene." By taking these stances, they can see each other, and most of their body and facial expressions can be viewed by the audience as well. Their voices also project out into the audience rather than into the wings (the backstage areas of the stage) or the "flies," the area of the stage housed above the acting area and out of the view of the audience, where scenery is "flown" in and out on batons. If actor 1 intentionally turns ¾ USL to actor 2, standing ¼ DSR and facing him, actor 1 is "giving him the stage."

It should be said here that many of these "rules" of staging are disregarded in the modern theater. Now that actors wear body mics, they can face any direction onstage and be heard by the audience. An embarrassing moment came once when an actor's mic was left on when he exited, and soon after the sound of a toilet flushing reverberated throughout the theater. This, of course, would not have been the case when Pamela Colman Smith was working in the theater.

Upstaging occurs when actor 1 stands in a ¼ R or ¼ L downstage position to actor 2, whom he is addressing. Actor 2 is standing in a ¾ R or ¾ L position upstage, facing him. This places the upstage actor 1 in a strong position to the audience and the downstage actor 2 in a weak position; his back is virtually to the audience. This is a cardinal sin in the theater if actor 1 does this deliberately in order to "steal the scene" from actor 2. In either case it is a power play. Actor 1 dominates actor 2.

(Theater note: I was once playing a scene with another actor in *The Would-Be Gentleman* by Molière. Each time he delivered his line to me, he took a step upstage, intending to "upstage me." This would cause me to turn my back to the audience to deliver my line. I, in turn, took one step upstage each time to meet him on his level. This continued until we had almost reached the back wall of the set. After our exit, we had a "discussion" about the scene we had just played. It wasn't played that way again!)

Actors rarely stand in profile R and L to each other. The most important part of the actor's instrument, his face, is only half seen, and his voice trails off into the wings. That is why actors do not like wearing an actual mask onstage. Their most important tool of expression has been covered. In lieu of three-dimensional masks, actors will paint a mask on their face with makeup. Then, at least, the muscles of the face can change expression and their expressive eyes can be seen to greater advantage.

When an actor stands full back to the audience, he is often in a heightened emotional state—either real or feigned. For example, the character in the Five of Cups may be silently grieving a loss, or perhaps proudly displaying the fruits of his labors, in the Ten of Cups.

All these positions will be referred to when the Minors are discussed. Pamela Colman Smith would have been very familiar with all these terms prior to her illustrating the pictures on the cards of the Waite-Smith Tarot deck.

Dominant Stage Positions
From Left to Right, Top to Bottom (see figure on page 40)

A. (Top row) Figures L and R are "sharing the scene." Neither is dominating.

B. Figure L is upstaging Figure R, requiring him to look upstage to her to deliver her lines.

C. (Second row) Figure L is being upstaged by Figure R, forcing her to look upstage to deliver her lines.

D. Figure R is taking himself out of the scene by turning his back and crossing downstage from Figure L.

E. (Third row) Though not illustrated in the diagram, keep in mind that body posture must be taken into consideration as well: standing on a platform is stronger than standing on a flat surface, which is stronger than stooping; stooping is stronger than bending at the waist, which is stronger than kneeling; kneeling is stronger than squatting to lying down, and so on.

Question: Which of the four characters here is dominating the stage? Why?

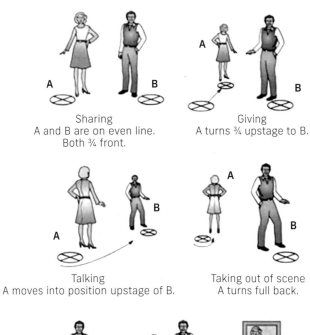

Sharing
A and B are on even line.
Both ¾ front.

Giving
A turns ¾ upstage to B.

Talking
A moves into position upstage of B.

Taking out of scene
A turns full back.

Character downstage right,
standing on an elevated platform,
takes focus.

Taking out of scene
A turns full back.

UPSTAGE RIGHT	UPSTAGE CENTER	UPSTAGE LEFT
STAGE RIGHT	STAGE CENTER	STAGE LEFT
DOWNSTAGE RIGHT	DOWNSTAGE CENTER	DOWNSTAGE LEFT

PROSCENIUM LINE

APRON

THE "STAGES OF YOUR LIFE" SPREAD BACKSTAGE

Exercise

Reflect on the formative years of your life in three "stages." After all, "All the world's a stage," so let's use what you've learned about stage positions to examine the "stages" or ages of your life. Shuffle the full deck and follow the spread that follows.

1. The Early Years:
   A. Place three cards in the downstage row from left to right.
   Question: What did you discover?

2. The Middle Years:
   A. Place three cards in the middle row from left to right.
   Question: What are you learning? Or did you learn?

3. The Later Years:
   A. Place three cards in the upstage row, from left to right.
   Question: How are you growing? Or did you grow?

4. Backstage.
   A. Place two cards above the chart: backstage.
   Question: Throughout your journey, who or what went on "backstage," behind the scenes, that supported you? That hindered you? (these may be public or private). Backstage sometimes carries with it a certain pejorative connotation, perhaps a detriment to your "onstage" life.

5. The Wings.
   A. Place one card to the left of the chart and to the right of the chart ("the Wings").
   Question: Who or what is waiting in the "wings?" SR to enter? Where will it take you? SL. We usually think of something positive entering from the wings, especially SR wing.

6. Life Goes On. Place one card on the table, backside up: "the Curtain Call" (do not show the face of the card). If you are satisfied with the answer from #5 above, leave the remaining card facedown. If you're feeling that you would like more information, turn the card over and discover what it holds for you. If you turn it over, it enters into the energy of your question. If you leave it upside down, the energy is not activated.

7.   Now write a brief synopsis of your life up to this point. Look for patterns, themes, recurring obstacles, strategies for success.

8.   Note: The "Stages of Your Life" spread can be adapted to any stage of your life in the same way (e.g., work, relationship, health, politics, environment, family, and so on).

Exercise

When time is limited, you may also lay out nine cards horizontally and read them as a scene in a play in which several characters are involved. The horizontal line need not be a straight one. You can place one card higher or lower or on the same level in relation to another to indicate your sense of their relative power or weakness (status). You can space the cards closely together or place gaps between them to indicate their relative connectiveness or lack thereof. Does it change the way you feel when you place two cards near each other or farther away? The closer the space, the more you may favor their proximity; farther apart likely indicates the degree to which you dislike their association. Notice the four examples below as separate entities, and observe how Smith tells part of the story by the distance she places between/among the characters. This is known as "spatial relationships." Can you think of other cards where space is an important element of the story?

Include as many parts of a well-written play as you can. Keep in mind that movement, posture, and direction are keys to the development and interpretation of the scene and the interrelationships among characters. Now write a story in narrative form in your journal or notebook as you interpret the spread you've created.

Your Story (record this in your journal or notebook)

THE MINOR CARDS

These cards are grouped by their commonality. Some cards fit into more than one category. They were placed in the group that was most applicable. The Golden Dawn titles appear below each card. These titles were likely first seen in MacGregor Mather's Book T around 1890 and later adapted by the Golden Dawn. We know that Smith was influenced by these titles; however, with few exceptions, the discussion will be confined to the relevance that her theater knowledge may have played in the rendering of these cards.

Characters that are entering, crossing, or looking from stage right to left or anticipating an entrance from SR

As mentioned before, this is a strong directional movement or stance onstage. This is often the case; it is not a law: SR—reflecting on the past or the current circumstance; SL—anticipating or imagining the future.

The Nine of Swords

THE LORD OF DESPAIR AND CRUELTY

We see a figure in bed with head bowed, face covered. This is a posture of grief, fear, a horror that literally cannot be faced. When we cannot face our fears, we often turn our backs to them. The character's back is to SR, where, in her imaginings, the source of the oncoming terror, the impending doom, or the heartbreaking memories are about to enter; these may be real, imagined, or part of a nightmare. The character is also sitting, leaning forward in bed with lower torso covered. This makes the figure even more vulnerable, unable to escape quickly. The character has become, at least in her mind, a victim with no way out. She is frozen and paralyzed by fear; we observe this in her overall aspect. The scene is darkly lit, with foreboding shadows lurking and bouncing about the room. Smith has created a world in this card to which we all have had the misfortune to visit at one time or another. The COVID-19 pandemic is an all-too-familiar example!

The Queen of Swords

QUEEN OF THE THRONES OF AIR

Our first impression may be a woman of authority because of her costume and crown. An elevated area has power onstage; she is sitting on a throne that is mounted on a dais. Because her power is implicit, there is no need for her to rise. Whether her adversary is without or within, she welcomes and faces it without hesitation. We see that in the open position of her body and her extended left arm. Her posture is erect. She holds a sword to remind us of her power and authority. However, it is held upright, so her power is more mental than physical. Her face is expressionless, giving nothing more away than she is willing to reveal. She welcomes the future as she faces stage left, where the future onstage generally resides. Her left hand is open, but with fingers held closely together; the hand held in this way sends a mixed message. We anticipate that she may be amenable to compromise, but she knows how far she will go when negotiating and will give nothing away gratuitously. The scene is outdoors. The atmosphere feels clean and fresh. She rises above the clouds, which may represent challenges she has overcome in her past. She is ready to move on.

The Six of Wands

THE LORD OF VICTORY

Smith signals in a number of ways that here is a man of power. Again, the figure is elevated, this time on a horse. Notice his erect posture, head held high, on the back of his steed. He is wearing a laurel wreath, a symbol of victory, and he is surrounded by a group of faithful followers, perhaps his devoted soldiers. From his wand also hangs a laurel wreath. If the rider is a warrior, we know that he has been victorious; he has shed his accoutrement of armor and is dressed in apparel to greet the admiring throngs. Even the horse looks over his downstage shoulder in obeisance to his master. We know that Smith was also a costumer, so the power of the color red of the cape conveys authority and passion, distinguishing him from others in the scene, who are of lesser status.

The Ten of Wands

THE LORD OF OPPRESSION

As referenced earlier, The Golden Dawn's titles will rarely be cited as a source of Smith's inspiration for her illustrations. However, this one is irresistible. There are many cards in the fifteenth-century Italian Sola Busca deck that show figures carrying a burdensome number of the symbols of their suit—in this instance, Wands; here, we see a man who is barely managing to keep the wands upright. This is surely Smith's source for the Ten of Wands. And we know that Waite recommended that she look at this deck for inspiration.

The character's back is to the audience. He is self-absorbed. The character's posture is also stooped with head bowed; we can imagine that he is undergoing some kind of physical or emotional burden, and perhaps he wants to make a show of it!

I quote Lena Horne, the late actress and song stylist:

There are those who are in love with responsibility. They are the classic workaholic, the martyr whose motto is "Do it all or it won't be done right." They complain but they wouldn't have it any other way. "It's not the load that breaks you down; it's the way you carry it."

I've often thought that if this character didn't want to draw attention to how hard he is working, he might carry the bundle of wands on his back . . . much easier that way, and he can see where he is going! But, he is headed in the right direction—stage left. Yes, this is also a stage card, so perhaps exaggeration is used here to make the point.

Page of Wands

THE PRINCESS OF THE SHINING FLAME:
The Rose of the Palace of Fire

This page has come into our view from SR and is now taking a pause on his journey before moving farther SL into the future. His posture is erect; his head is directed upward toward his goal. He is young. He is optimistic and bound-lessly curious. This is a "Look out, world; here I come" stance. There is something quirky about the feather adorning his hat. Smith may be suggesting with a wink that he is a

PAGE of WANDS.

character who does things his way. His US foot is slightly ahead of the one DS. This would indicate that he is balanced and about to take his next step. An actor often leads with his US foot, and exits on a diagonal from US to DS. This is a stronger position that keeps him more open to the audience.

The Six of Cups

THE LORD OF PLEASURE

In theatrical staging, as previously stated, the position in which we find these two characters is called "Sharing the scene." This means that they are facing each other in a ¼ L and ¼ R stance. In this way, they can relate to each other and remain open to the audience. The seemingly older character has a prop—in this case a flower, and his body is inclined in an act of giving. The younger character is just noticeably downstage of the other. This tells us that the older character is the dominant of the two at this moment. Rather than suggesting pleasant memories of times gone by, the traditional meaning of this card, some believe, is possibly a dark side. Notice that the girl has not extended her US hand to receive the flowers; that may suggest something offered that is unwanted. Looking more closely, Smith seems to have drawn two faces on the girl, or so it appears: one facing the boy, where she seems to be smiling, and one shown in her hair, where she looks disturbed. Perhaps that is her protector seen exiting USR, or was he the aggressor and the boy who remains her protector? In its lower polarity, this card may signal unwanted advances and more.

The Eight of Cups

THE LORD OF ABANDONED SUCCESS

The character is exiting USL. This telegraphs a great deal about the nature of the exit. The red cloak immediately attracts attention. It signals his passion and determination. He crosses SL over a rugged terrain. The fact that he is moving in that direction at all (SR→SL) signals an intention or plan for the future. He is leaving for a reason. (In actor shorthand, this would look like "X DSR→USL.")

Crossing the mountains ahead will pose another challenge. He is moving to higher ground, both literally and figuratively. That is where his gaze seems to be focused. (Actors love working on a set with levels! It is the child in them that delights in play!) But why is he leaving a life that seems perfectly in order? Perhaps he has done all he can do there. Has it become mundane and monotonous? He cannot resist the challenge; it is what he requires to remain vital and alive. Perhaps he is a physician leaving a successful practice at home to join "Doctors Without Borders."

The Knight of Pentacles

KNIGHT of PENTACLES.

THE LORD OF THE WIDE AND FERTILE LAND:
The King of the Spirits of Earth

We find this young knight in armor with his visor raised. Rather than a lance, he is holding the symbol of his suit. Though all dressed up, for the moment he does not appear to have any place to go—not for now at least. All four legs of the horse are in contact with the earth. This suggests stability. His facial expression, as he surveys the landscape, signals that he is thoughtfully contemplating his mission before he proceeds.

When he does move, we see that Smith has positioned him to move SL. That direction onstage shows strength and suggests that he intends to fulfill his mission after weighing it carefully. The landscape also lends credence to this idea of waiting. It looks as though the furrowed fields have been plowed. It would be reasonable to assume that the land has also been seeded. The crop will break through the soil, and it will soon be time to reap its harvest. Perhaps "all things do come to those who wait" . . . after the investment has been made!

The Knight of Cups

KNIGHT of CUPS.

THE LORD OF THE WAVES AND THE WATERS:
The King of the Hosts of the Sea

In this card, we see another knight. We have preconceived notions about how a knight should look and behave. Smith knew how to costume him in armor and, like knights in the Sola Busca, this knight is on horseback. However, unlike most knights, he is not charging off into battle; we see that his visor is up, he has no weapon that is visible, he wears no gloves, and he is carrying a cup. By observing the gait of the horse, we can tell that the knight is moving slowly but with intention. From what we can see from his face, he appears to be young, as we would expect in his role as knight; he sits up high and erect in the saddle. This signals to us that he is strong and ready to fulfill his mission. Perhaps he will bring new life to a rather parched-looking terrain. Since his suit is Cups, this may come in the form of love to a world that has lost sight of the worth and equality of its fellow man.

The Five of Pentacles

THE LORD OF MATERIAL TROUBLE

Smith has dressed these two figures in rags; the boy is crippled, assisted by crutches, and perhaps suffering from leprosy. Notice he is wearing a bell around his neck; this is a way of warning others to keep their distance. Here is an example of where props are telling an important part of the story; they may be mother and son. Smith has telegraphed a relationship between them in the costumes they are wearing. In both costumes we see the colors blue and yellow; the fabrics on both are polka-dotted. This is an example of "color coding," indicating that they are related in some way. The woman is barefoot and her posture is stooped, and, in this scene, snow is falling and settling on the ground. Miss Smith has created a bleak picture for sure. It appears that they are unaware of the church as they cross SL. Perhaps the church is not a beacon of refuge for them as it may be for others. However, it is encouraging that they are moving at all under the circumstances, and they are moving in a strong direction, from SR to SL. Their survival instincts are stronger than their current state of desperation. We have been given reason to believe that there are better days ahead. Not all is lost.

PAGE of PENTACLES.

Page of Pentacles

THE PRINCESS OF THE ECHOING HILLS:
The Rose of the Palace of Earth

There is something whimsical in the way that Smith has drawn the Page of Pentacles. We could almost imagine that he is a ballet dancer, with his right leg extended gracefully behind him. He has a certain spring in his step, as we might expect from a young page. He is gazing at the pentacle that he holds up in front of him with an all-consuming interest. The body posture does not suggest that he's ready to act on it, but it has his attention, and we can expect that he will be on the move soon. For the moment, he's in love with the idea that has captured his fascination. He is a page, after all, and we know that pages are messengers as well as students, so this is just a pause. Notice in the background the same furrowed land that we observed in the Knight of Pentacles card, but at a farther distance. He will tend to planting his ideas when the time comes.

The Eight of Pentacles

THE LORD OF PRUDENCE

Smith has illustrated a young man who appears to be devoted to his work. His posture is inclined over his pentacles, but not bent or stooped. His DS leg is extended and his US leg slightly behind as he straddles his workbench. This gives him good balance and enables him to stay comfortably focused on his work for a good length of time. He is young; his facial expression conveys pure satisfaction as he gives his full concentration to making these pentacles. His costume tells us that he is a tradesman, not a craftsman. We know that because each pentacle is identical. Smith has costumed him wearing a leather apron over the very simple clothing of a commoner. Once again, we have another example of a stage card. The backdrop reveals the town in the distance. Is there a disconnect between the work that he is doing and the community it's meant to serve? Or is he devoted to his work out of his very need to provide for the commonwealth?

The Six of Swords

THE LORD OF EARNED SUCCESS

Once again, Smith has a wonderful ability to tell stories with her pictures. It's sometimes like watching a silent movie. Here we see a group of three figures. One is higher than the other two. We've seen this configuration in a number of her cards: the Hierophant, the Lovers, the Chariot, the Devil, Death, Judgement, the Three of Pentacles and the Six of Pentacles. In all these cards, the superior figure has power or status over the lower figures. In the Six of Swords, we see a man standing in a boat; he appears strong as he maneuvers the boat with his pole. His posture is erect. The two lower figures are covered and leaning forward, indicating vulnerability and a need to be rescued from their current situation. The boat is moving SL, which tells us that they are en route to a future better than the past that they are leaving behind. Smith's Christian faith may have informed some aspects of this card. They appear to be leaving unsettled waters to calmer seas. In Psalms 23, it reads in part, "He leadeth me beside the still waters." Perhaps, more descriptively, he is leading them into still waters from waters that appear disturbed. The image is also reminiscent of the Holy Family: Jesus, Mary, and Joseph. We do not see all of the boat, which may indicate that the journey has just begun.

QUEEN of WANDS.

Queen of Wands

THE QUEEN OF THE THRONES OF FLAME

When Smith drew this court card, we already knew by her title that she was in a position of authority. She is sitting center stage, full front, and on a throne, and the throne is raised on a platform. Again, height brings with it power and strength. The Queen is quite comfortable as she rules confidently from her throne. The lions on her throne are looking SR and SL. This would suggest that she rules fairly, since she considers both sides of the issue presented to her. However, she does not suffer fools gladly. We notice the black cat who sits at the Queen's feet FF, with a stare that can see through any falsehood. Smith distinguishes this queen from others in the deck. The colors in the card are reds, oranges, and yellows. This communicates warmth, energy, and passion. Her legs are widely spread; this could indicate that she possesses certain masculine traits, or that she is comfortable acknowledging her sexuality. She is looking in the direction of DSL. Perhaps she has just given audience to a subject who is exiting the stage. As a sidenote, it has been said that this card is modeled after Edy Craig, daughter of Ellen Terry and likely intimate of Pamela Smith's (Katz and Goodwin 2015).

The Three of Pentacles

THE LORD OF MATERIAL WORKS

Here we have another example of three characters, one on a higher level, standing on a bench, and two standing on the floor, appearing to be deferring to him. The figure on the bench is in a dominant position. It appears as though he is a craftsman who is working on these Gothic arches. Plans are important, but finally, they remain on paper unless there are craftsmen and workmen to execute them. We know that he is at work, because the props in his hands are tools that appear to be designed for chiseling stone. Props also have a way of telling us something about the character. Costumes and props in this card advance the story. They each delineate the role of the three figures: a craftsman, a member of the clergy, and perhaps the architect who is holding the plans. It also shows an interdependence among the three: each is necessary to complete the work.

KING of CUPS.

King of Cups

THE PRINCE OF THE CHARIOT
OF THE WATERS

There is a certain sense of resignation that the King of Cups conveys as he sits, facing nearly FF on his throne, holding the symbol of his suit and a scepter, a symbol of his authority. The water around him is far from calm. He precariously steadies himself with legs apart and SR foot extended for balance. The colors of his costume suggest the duality of his personality. The reds and yellows of his cape denote the power of his office, while a light-blue robe drapes his body, suggesting a sort of coolness and sensitivity. He focuses his attention SL, surveying his kingdom. Despite the unrest that surrounds him, he is duty bound to perform the duties of his office, but he may not be best suited for that role. He might rather be engaged in some creative endeavor or serving in the role of an understanding and compassionate counselor. Perhaps he is the "king who would be man."

CHAPTER SIX

CHARACTERS FACING OR MOVING STAGE RIGHT

The following cards show characters who are facing or moving SR. This may indicate that they anticipate an entrance, either friend or foe from that direction; they may also may be taking time to reflect before moving forward. Often, if a character looks or moves SR, he looks to where he has been; if a character looks or moves to SL, he looks to where he is going (again, this is a tendency, not a rule; still, it is frequently the case).

The Five of Swords

THE LORD OF DEFEAT

There is something unsettling in this card's scenery and costume. There are dark clouds in the sky, the water is choppy, and the DS character's green tunic along with his hair seems to be moved by the wind blowing in from SR. He looks over his SR right shoulder at the two men in the background who are crossing US and away from him. He may be anticipating that they will return and continue the fight. It doesn't look as though he is in any imminent danger though. He's rather weighted down by the swords he is carrying, and the sword in his US hand is pointed downward. He believes the fight is over. This is also another of the stage cards. Does the DS character think he has won but in fact has lost? "For what price glory?" But for now, he is in a dominant DS position. The other two characters appear to be walking away in defeat; their backs are to us as they cross US.

The Seven of Swords

THE LORD OF UNSTABLE EFFORT

In this stage card, we see a character carrying swords and looking over his SL shoulder. It appears he is crossing SR whence he came, checking perhaps to see if he is being followed. His gait and the position of his legs look as though he is attempting to move rather stealthily. Is he stealing those swords or retrieving what is rightfully his to reclaim? If he is a thief, he may be fairly new at it; the Golden Dawn title suggests that his efforts are "unstable." The bright palette of colors that Smith uses in the costume and scenery tells us that nothing terribly serious is going on. The expression on his face telegraphs that he's rather enjoying the success of his crafty maneuver. Perhaps he doesn't have far to go. Those swords are heavy and are going to weigh him down if he is not relieved of them in short order.

Page of Swords

THE PRINCESS OF THE RUSHING WINDS:
The Lotus of the Palace of Air

In this card, we see a page in a stance that also suggests a position from a ballet. In this case, the sword is a prop and is not meant to be viewed as a weapon. Her head is higher than the billowy, white clouds on the backdrop. She stands on a mound of earth that gives her more height. Does this suggest that she is aloof and above it all? She is looking over her DSR shoulder, hair blowing in the wind; she appears interested in who or what may be entering from SR to interrupt her "dance." She is taking time out from her duties as a page and enjoying the luxuries of youth and the open air, as she revels in thought.

Knight of Swords

THE LORD OF THE WIND AND THE BREEZES:
The King of the Spirits of Air

KNIGHT of SWORDS.

Is this Knight tearing off to do battle with a foe? It's hard to say. His visor is raised. But he is definitely "in the moment" (an acting term, meaning fully present and focused on an intention). Notice how he leans into the scene with sword raised. In terms of stage movement, crossing from SL to SR is not so strong a direction as entering from SR. If he is engaging with an opponent charging from SR, this might suggest a battle that will not go in his favor. He is riding against the wind. We see the jagged clouds in the background and the trees bending toward him on the backdrop. He clearly likes challenges but spends little time in planning. Perhaps that is why we see only half of the horse; he is in process. However, there is a fierce sense of determination in his facial expression. Winning is better than losing, but not fighting at all is simply not an option.

The Two of Wands

THE LORD OF DOMINION

We can tell from the costume and the setting that this man is of the upper classes. His erect posture and what we can see of his face tells us that he is a younger man. At first, it may look as though we are observing a man who expresses an air of self-confidence. But why does he hold on to a wand in his left hand and a globe in his right; further, the wand to his right is tethered to the battlement wall, which also provides protection and stability for him. Even more telling is the fact that he is looking SR but shows no inclination to move. This sometimes indicates that the character is reflecting on the past, perhaps past successes, remembering what was or what might have been and longing for more.

The Nine of Wands

THE LORD OF GREAT STRENGTH

The figure standing with head bandaged and leaning on a pole for support has clearly been wounded. Whether he has been physically, emotionally, or psychologically wounded can be debated. We do see that he is standing in front of a fortification of Wands. He knows he has his back covered—a good strategy for any combatant; it may also indicate that he has developed unfounded paranoia. "Better safe than sorry." He is looking intently off SR. In our earlier discussion, we said that important entrances are more often made from SR. In this case, he may be anticipating the return of the threat and is ready to defend himself. His facial expression belies a certain fearful anticipation. Perhaps he is over-exaggerating this threat. He is apparently standing on a stage, the place where reality to the character may sometimes be a mere illusion. But he does appear to be young, strong, and capable of taking on his adversary, should he be forced to engage.

Knight of Wands

THE LORD OF THE FLAME AND LIGHTING:
The King of the Spirits of Fire

Behind his raised visor, this knight's facial expression reveals a rather callow youth. Men are generally knighted at the age of twenty-one. He appears ready to charge into battle, with his strong, rearing steed eager and ready to take him there—whether there's a mission to pursue or not: "Let me at 'em!" Sometimes a young warrior can "rush in where angels fear to tread" for the sheer love of adventure and the lack of experience; these attributes may give him a false sense of confidence and protection. Something or someone has captured his attention off SR; he may see his opponent charging in his direction. Tempering his headstrong nature, combined with more experience in battle, may transform him into the emissary of rescue that he is meant to be. Right now, he's all dressed up and just wants to enter into the fray, perhaps to be the first to rescue the damsel in distress. "Once more, unto the breach!" as he heads off in all directions. The 45° angle of the horse's body may also be intended as a phallic symbol. Wands is the most sexual of the suits.

King of Wands

THE PRINCE OF THE CHARIOT OF FIRE

KING of WANDS.

The King of Wands is sitting erect on his raised throne and looking off SR. His facial expression conveys keen interest. He may be anticipating the entrance of someone he's expecting, but he takes nothing for granted. He is ready to act at a moment's notice. Observe how he leans slightly forward on his throne. Holding his wand in his right hand, with his left hand resting on his thigh, he is prepared to rise. His feet are unencumbered by his fiery-red robe that matches his flaming-red hair. His mantle is draped behind him, freeing him for action, another indication that he is more than a king in title (we will see the mantle worn this way by all the kings except for the King of Pentacles). He is every bit a ruler who is in charge of his kingdom and more than equipped to discharge the powers that he is privileged by his position.

The Two of Cups

THE LORD OF LOVE

The two characters in this scene, as cited in the introduction, may have been inspired by the play Romeo and Juliet. It is, again, a stage card. The focus here is on the male character, because he is facing SR and attending to the female character, who may have entered from that direction. His body language tells us that he is taking the lead. His US hand reaches out to touch hers, and his DS foot is taking a step forward. She stands receptive but is still. Notice too that they are standing in a ¼ L and ¼ R relationship to each other, another example of "sharing the scene."

The chalices or props in their hands are about to meet in a toast, showing a bond or agreement between the two. One would expect that Smith would have used color coding in the costumes if this were exclusively a romantic relationship. We can gather, therefore, that it insinuates any kind of agreeable relationship.

Page of Cups

THE PRINCESS OF THE WATERS:
The Lotus of the Palace of the Floods

PAGE of CUPS.

The Page of Cups is gazing quizzically at a fish that is peering out of the chalice he is holding. His balanced stance on this stage card, his feet a distance apart with his left fist on his waist, gives us the impression that he has paused there for a while to make some sense of it. It doesn't appear to be an urgent matter, but rather a source of youthful curiosity for this impressionable page. He may be asking himself, "What is the message here?" One may also assume from his flowery tunic and rather decorous hat, with sash draped "devil may care" over his right shoulder, that he is a creative trendsetter, rather than one who goes along with the establishment.

Queen of Cups

THE QUEEN OF THE THRONES
OF THE WATERS

QUEEN of CUPS.

The Queen of Cups appears surer of herself than her consort, the King. This is indicated by Smith in the two contrasting settings. The King is surrounded by rough seas with no land in sight. While the Queen, on the other hand, is near water, but her feet are planted firmly on dry land. The water around her is virtually still. The Queen's imagination is piqued as she gazes intently at this rather mysterious-looking cup, a cup unlike any other we've seen in the suit. It bears a striking resemblance to a monstrance used in the Catholic church to house and display holy relics. (Perhaps this is an homage to Smith's Catholic religion to which she converted in 1911. She even took the middle name Mary.) When we place the cards side by side, we can see that Smith was working with color coding to connect the King and Queen. She has used blues, yellows, and reds in their costumes. The King's palette employs more-saturated color, while hers trends toward the pastels. They each have their role to play, and they work together compatibly. Perhaps his "rule" of the kingdom is more a sense of duty rather than a desire for power. The cup holds a powerful place in this illustration since it is SR of the Queen and has captured her attention. Perhaps she is contemplating how its contents may hold the key to her ascending the throne of her consort. For now, she is weighing her options.

The Six of Pentacles

THE LORD OF MATERIAL SUCCESS

Here, once again, we see a pyramid of figures that Smith often uses in the deck to show relationships among characters and, often, one's status over the other two. We also see a connection by means of the color palette: the beggar SR wears a yellow cloak, which matches the yellow in the nobleman's boots; the beggar SL is in blue, which ties in with the blue strips of the nobleman's tunic. Smith's center character stands above the two who are kneeling. She has costumed him in the clothes of a nobleman. His posture is erect. His attention now is on the beggar kneeling SR. The beggar facing SL and receiving the coins is in a ¼ L position to the nobleman. This opens him to the audience and gives him focus. The beggar in blue is facing SR in a ¾ USR position to the nobleman. This is all to show that the nobleman is in a position of power. His props are coins, which he is giving to the beggar; the hand holding the coins is in the same position we see with the Magician and the Hierophant in the Majors, except, in this case, his hand is held upside down. Is this meant to be a blessing in the form of money? His facial expression belies an air of benevolence. The beggars are humbly dressed in rags and leaning toward him. The fact that it is a stage card may cause us to question the authenticity of his generosity or the sincerity of the beggars' needs. To query what at first seems obvious gives this card greater depth of meaning as one interprets it.

The Seven of Pentacles

THE LORD OF SUCCESS UNFULFILLED

This young man thoughtfully looks SR at his vines, while leaning on a hoe. Since the vines are SR of the character, we can assume that he is assessing work accomplished. His legs are spread rather far apart; this stance suggests that he may have been in this position for some time. Is he resting and enjoying the toils of his labors, or does he feel that the crop fails to measure up to his expectations? The plants appear healthy, but they are not bearing fruit. The sky is gray; some of the leaves on the vines are brown, as is the hilly landscape behind him. The Golden Dawn title "The Lord of Success Unfulfilled" may influence our choice, as surely Smith was aware. In any case, it does seem as though the character's life, for the moment, is at a standstill.

Queen of Pentacles

THE QUEEN OF THE THRONES OF EARTH

This Queen sits on her throne, which is located outdoors on a dais of earth. Flowers grow abundantly around her feet; a trellis of flowers frames her from above. She appears to be quite at home in nature. She holds her pentacle almost as adoringly as a mother would cradle her newborn. Her body leans into the pentacle; her facial expression displays a loving attentiveness. Smith costumes her in a red robe. Beneath her calm exterior, there is a passion to protect and defend those who are in her charge, especially her children. She is sitting in a ¼ R position. She may be reflecting on sweet memories of the past or experiencing the melancholy of the "empty-nest syndrome." She is at her best when she can be the one who nurtures. She would not make a good patient.

CHARACTERS ISOLATED FROM THE WORLD AROUND THEM, FACING FULL FRONT

The Two of Swords

THE LORD OF PEACE RESTORED

The woman, blindfolded and dressed in a white robe, sits in front of a painted backdrop of blue sky, bathed in the light of a crescent-shaped moon overhead. The water ripples behind her. It may be dawn. Dawn is often associated with a reawakening. Her arms are crossed over her heart chakra. Perhaps she is protecting herself from further hurt. Her blindfold serves as a barrier to keep the world at bay. She has gone within; perhaps she is meditating. The result of this kind of introspection may restore needed balance in her life. She is sitting FF. As previously stated, FF is also the most vulnerable of all body postures. She may be less protected, but she is also more open to what message may await her from within. There is always a risk when one goes seeking her inner truth.

The white robe, combined with the swords, clearly not meant to be used as weapons at this moment, suggests that she may be participating in a kind of induction ceremony. Maybe she is weighing the better of two options. Though there is tension in the upper body from balancing the heavy swords, her legs appear relaxed and open. She is prepared to wait for the message to manifest.

The Eight of Swords

THE LORD OF SHORTENED FORCE

The woman, blindfolded and loosely wrapped in ties suggesting self-limiting beliefs, is standing in front of a backdrop of eight swords and, farther in the background, a castle. There is an opening in the swords, providing a way back in or a way out. From her wrinkled garment and disheveled hair, it appears that her journey has been anything but smooth. If she returns, all that binds her will remain. If she moves forward, there is no certainty that life will improve; DS of her is a swampy landscape—a rough road lies ahead. However, she has taken a small step forward, tentative though it may be. This is a good indication that she is attempting to leave her life of isolation and intimidation behind in search of a more nurturing community. She is moving in the right direction. It is interesting that Smith has drawn the figure standing between two groups of swords: a group of five that are upstage of her—what she is leaving behind—and a group of three, one of which is DS of her, which is what she is moving toward. This is consistent with what we know about most of the fives and threes in the RWS deck—being cut off from community (the 5s) and, conversely, moving to become part of it (the 3s). As she gains more confidence, she will learn to shed those ties that barely bind her.

The Four of Pentacles

THE LORD OF EARTHLY POWER

In this stage card, we see similarities with the Two of Swords. They both are sitting on a bench, FF with arms crossed over the heart chakra. They both hold symbols of their suit, but that is where the likenesses end. By the quality of his robe, his mantle, and his crown, we see that he is a king. He may feel he has nothing but his title and his possessions to protect him, so he holds on to them tenaciously. He seems unaware of his kingdom, which appears diminutively on the backdrop behind him. His self-interests are all that concern him at the moment. We may conclude at times that a character who sits or stands FF is telling us that "It's all about me."

This card continues to remain relevant in that regard. We find leaders today who manifest some of those qualities.

The Four of Cups

THE LORD OF BLENDED PLEASURE

In the previous two cards, we saw characters who embrace their suits. Here, in the Four of Cups, we see a character who is ignoring or rejecting his. The cup that is coming in from a cloud, if taken literally, is clearly in his peripheral vision, but it seems to go unnoticed. He is sitting FF, and once again his arms are crossed over his heart chakra. His eyes appear to be closed; his facial expression seems relaxed. Perhaps we should not read too much into this card. It is conceivable that he is just taking some time for himself. He may be gazing at the three cups before him and taking stock of his past accomplishments. Meditation may assist him in taking those next steps. The cup appearing from a cloud may contain his next lesson. The cup clearly takes focus since it enters the scene from SR. It is in motion, as opposed to the young man, who appears in stasis, for now at least.

"When the student is ready, the teacher will appear" (quote attributed to the Theosophical Society).

The Nine of Cups

THE LORD OF MATERIAL HAPPINESS

Smith shows us a man who appears quite satisfied; it would be hard to imagine that he's ever missed a meal. The nine cups behind him tells us that liquid refreshment is well stocked. Smith's rendering may imply that he's also quite full of himself. He sits on a bench, arms crossed over his chest and legs spread, FF to the audience. In *Bringing the Tarot to Life: Embody the Cards through Creative Exploration*, I wrote that with his heart chakra closed and his legs spread, casual sex may be one way to interpret this card. His facial expression tells us that all is well . . . for now. Abundance is the source of his happiness, but overindulgence may lead to his undoing.

CHAPTER EIGHT

CHARACTERS WITH BACKS TO THE AUDIENCE

They appear isolated in their world of thought and contemplation.
The focus lies in what has captured their attention.

The Seven of Cups

THE LORD OF ILLUSORY SUCCESS

Characters whose backs are to the audience in a stationary position are usually preoccupied in thought. Sometimes they are waiting, and at other times mourning, or celebrating their accomplishments, as the family is doing in the Ten of Cups. They are not interacting with other characters, nor are they doing anything to move the plot forward. They are temporarily at a standstill and must decide before they can move on.

We can interpret little about this character, because his back is to us in black silhouette. Only a portion of his body is captured in the scene. Our focus is drawn to what he sees before him; the message comes from where his gaze is fixed. He extends his right hand to the cups in a gesture that suggests indecisiveness. He may be so overwhelmed by his choices that he pleads for them to decide for him. The shawled figure outlined in red seems to be vying for his attention, though it looks as though he's concentrating on the cup over his right shoulder. Is he torn between earthly riches and the blessings of spirit? Timing often plays a key role when one is weighing his options. He may not be ready to heed his highest calling. Often when there are so many choices available, one is stymied by abundance.

The Five of Cups

THE LORD OF LOSS IN PLEASURE

This figure cloaked in black, standing erect and head bowed, is clearly in mourning. The world seems to stand still at times like these. Smith shows him a way out by way of the bridge in the distance. There he can rejoin his friends and the community where a source of support awaits, but he is not ready. Grief takes as long as it takes, and, for many, it must be done alone. The bridge will always be there. The cups behind him may be the opportunities that he's blind to at the moment. They too will be there when healing has taken its natural course. Notice that they are located SL. If he turns around and sees the cups behind him, he may pick them up and move into a future with more promise. On the other hand, he may remain fixed and immobilized by his lingering sorrow. Time does not heal all wounds, but it helps.

The Three of Wands

THE LORD OF ESTABLISHED STRENGTH

We see the back of a man standing on a cliff and looking out at sea. His costume suggests that he is an accomplished man of station, perhaps a tradesman or merchant, invested in securing his future. Take note of the ships in the water, which have captured his attention. Movement in a scene usually takes focus. The boats are moving from SL to SR. We may wonder why they are of such interest to him. Perhaps he has sent them on a mission, and they are returning with the bounty. We feel the anticipation of the ships' docking. It is also interesting to note that the color palette that Smith has used in this card. The Three of Wands is bathed in warm, rich colors. The costume of the man is a vibrant orange/red. The card vibrates with positive energy that he has poured into this endeavor, and now he waits. He is actively waiting, unlike the figure in the Seven of Cups or the Two of Wands. Sometimes, it is important to be patient and give our investments time to yield their reward.

The Ten of Cups

THE LORD OF PERFECTED SUCCESS

Smith has drawn the parents with their backs to us, as they survey their home and their land; the children look as though they are playing "Ring around the Rosie." This is the picture of the "perfect family." A rainbow of abundance frames and protects them from above. The focus is not on them, however, but on the fruits of their loving devotion to the land, their home, and their children. In another example of a stage card, we see that Smith has used color coding in the costumes to show connections among the members of the family. The taller girl is wearing orange and yellow, like her father; the smaller girl is wearing blue, like both of the parents.

There is also a shadow side to this stage card, which can signal that things are not always as they may appear. If Smith indeed meant to suggest "Ring around the Rosie," then there is irony in the children's folk rhyme. By one account, it is actually about the Great Plague of 1665 in London. Smith would have known of this rhyme; it is still chanted by children today. And since this is a ten, the end of a cycle, this may not always be "the perfect family." But, in most cases, this is a very happy card. If it shows up reversed, one might expect a family in conflict.

The Ten of Pentacles

THE LORD OF WEALTH

In the Ten of Pentacles, we have another kind of family, quite different from the one in the Ten of Cups. What Smith may have been alluding to here is revealed in the physical juxtaposition of the characters and the color coding in the costumes. Notice the body language of the married couple. Her facial expression as she looks at her husband reflects concern. This is not an expression of love and devotion. It seems that he is talking to her but is not looking at her. They are separated from the older man, seated outside the archway; his back is to us and cut off from those inside the arch. The couple could be engaging in a conversation that is not meant to be overheard. The woman and the older gentleman seem related by the red in both of their costumes, perhaps father and daughter.

The young man, dressed in blue, coordinates with the blue in the costume of the young boy. The dogs, symbols of devotion, are white, as are the hair and beard of the old man. He reaches out and pets one of the dogs. The attention of the child, a symbol of innocence, is also directed toward the dogs. The child, the elderly man, and the dogs have their own unique relationship. Is the couple discussing the long-awaited inheritance? Take note of the scenery as well. Outside the arch, it is gray and dull, save for patches of red; inside the arch, the sun is shining and the sky is an azure blue. This is one of the richest cards in the deck in terms of imagining the story. This unconventional interpretation is not the generally accepted meaning. It usually speaks of wealth and prosperity.

CHARACTERS FACING THE AUDIENCE IN A FULL, OPEN, FRONT POSITION

This often conveys a sense of power, accomplishment, satisfaction, and self-confidence, with nothing to hide.

KING of SWORDS.

King of Swords

THE PRINCE OF THE CHARIOT OF THE WINDS

The King of Swords is sitting on his throne in FF position. This is a powerful position. All of the actor's instrument (as an actor's body is called) is in full view and available to express what he is feeling and thinking. His mantle is open with nothing to hide. His light-blue robe matches the color of the sky. His sword is held more like a scepter than a weapon. Often, in Smith's landscapes, she paints jagged clouds and trees blowing in the wind. Here, however, the clouds are billowy and the trees are still. The King's left hand rests comfortably on his thigh; his legs appear relaxed. His facial expression is serious but not stern. His demeanor belies an air of composure and self-confidence. If we were to come before him in judgment, we could expect an honest and fair verdict.

The Nine of Pentacles

THE LORD OF MATERIAL GAIN

This woman is costumed in a style that tells us that she is a lady of wealth. She stands in her garden vineyard, which is boasting a bountiful crop of succulent grapes. The thick vines also serve as a wall that is nearly as high as her shoulders. She is separated from the community, which is seen as barely more than a speck on the backdrop behind her.

She is well protected, even from the falcon perched on her gloved left hand. Her facial expression conveys a sense of contentment. The color palette that Smith employs here is composed of the bright yellows and verdant greens of a healthy, fruit-bearing vineyard (contrast this with the vines barren of fruit in the Seven of Pentacles). The lady is surrounded by abundance, which we often associate with the privileged class. Though she is alone, she appears to be at peace with the compromises that she may have made in order to acquire what she has attained.

KING of PENTACLES.

King of Pentacles

THE PRINCE OF THE CHARIOT OF EARTH

This King is not likely to rise from his throne anytime soon. He is sitting on the most decorous of all the kings' thrones. If his left foot is any indication, he appears to be wearing armor under bulky and cumbersome robes as well. All in all, he is the most ostentatious of the kings. Much of his presentation is for show and proof of the abundance, bestowed upon him for his work and his sovereign authority. His facial expression conveys a sense of contemplation. Is he considering that even more would be better, or is he feeling contented with what he has? For the moment, his focus is not on his kingdom or his subjects. Painted on the backdrop USL is a portion of the town. A wall separates the King from his community. He may be a king of some standing, but at this stage of his later life, he is taking time off and enjoying the spoils of his labors. One might rightly assume now that his attention is on his immediate surroundings and the treasure trove of his possessions, which provide safety, security, and comfort for himself and his family.

VII

The Seven of Wands

THE LORD OF VALOR

Again, I believe that Smith was influenced by the Golden Dawn title when she illustrated this card, "The Lord of Valor." Here, we clearly see a brave and courageous young man determined to face great danger in battle single-handedly. His body is in a defensive position: his legs are spread wide to maintain balance. Standing on an elevated piece of land places him at a distinct advantage; however, both feet—one shoed in a slipper, the other in a boot—are very near the edge, so he is literally on a slippery slope. His facial expression denotes fear and a heightened sense of urgency as he defends himself against his adversaries. He is acutely aware that he is in a particularly precarious predicament. He holds his wand with a tight grip, determined to maintain control of his claim. The outcome is uncertain at the moment, but we are encouraged to cheer him on, because of his sheer determination.

The Two of Pentacles

THE LORD OF HARMONIOUS CHANGE

Juggling requires focus and concentration, certainly essential in order for an actor to be "in the moment." It is, after all, another of the stage cards. Painted on the backdrop, we see ships that are being tossed to and fro on the rocky seas. This character appears to be dancing all the while, seemingly oblivious to what is going on behind him; he is simply going with the flow. One is reminded of Nero, who fiddled while Rome was burning. His facial expression reveals that he is completely absorbed in the joy that juggling provides him. While his balance may be precarious, that does not seem to concern him now. He is looking at the pentacle in his SL hand; his next step is going to be with his SL foot. The tilt of his head and his gaze are in that direction as well. Generally, this would tend to suggest that the character is headed in the right direction. There's no great drama that's about to ensue here. He seems to be enjoying his "time-out." Tomorrow is another day. Smith has given us a light-blue background without a cloud in the sky. Even the colors in his costume are picked up by the colors in the SL ship on the horizon. There is no imminent threat. "The trick in juggling, however, is knowing when the balls are made of rubber and when they are made of glass" (*Bringing the Tarot to Life: Embody the Cards through Creative Exploration*).

CARDS THAT PRESENT WITHOUT CHARACTERS ILLUSTRATED

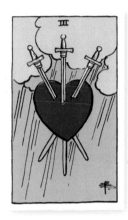

The Three of Swords

THE LORD OF SORROW

Excluding the four Aces, the Three of Swords is one of two cards in the Rider-Smith deck that does not include a human figure. There is no doubt that this is the closest Smith came to copying a card in the Sola Busca deck, though in that deck the card is much more ornate. The impact of this image is so powerful that Smith may have decided it could not be improved upon by including a character in the rendering. As I study this card, and I'm sure this was not Smith's intention, but, in keeping with the theater analogy, I see it as perhaps a painted backdrop for a ballet of Romeo and Juliet—the two outer swords representing the two lovers, and the center sword, the feud of their families that separated them. There is no escaping the fact that this is a card of Sorrow.

The Eight of Wands

THE LORD OF SWIFTNESS

If we want to think of these wands as literal wands, rather than just symbols of swiftness, we can imagine that they are being powerfully hurled from off SR. The wand throwers are implicit. Think of the Seven of Wands. We have no trouble believing that there are adversaries holding those wands, just out of sight at the bottom of the hill. That is because we have a character above to give them context. The Eight of Wands still has a story to tell. On the backdrop, we see a home on the horizon, virtually the same landscape we see in the

Ace of Wands. There is a river separating the land it's built on from the land in the foreground. The wands we see may be in the act of defending the home. Speed may suggest that time is of the essence in protecting this property. There is a plan and order behind the attack. The wands are not hurled randomly through the air but are launched in perfectly parallel flight and headed decisively toward their intended target, just out of our vision. Of the four suits, we ordinarily think of the Swords as weapons of defense, but we have also seen the Wands used for that purpose as well (i.e., the Five of Wands, the Seven of Wands, and, to some extent, the Nine of Wands). This could also represent the best outcome of a committee working together harmoniously: all on the same page and moving toward a commonly agreed-upon outcome.

THE ACES

The Ace of Wands

ROOT OF THE
POWERS OF FIRE

The Ace of Swords

ROOT OF THE
POWERS OF AIR

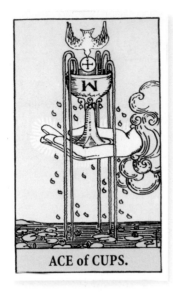

ACE of CUPS.

ACE of PENTACLES.

The Ace of Cups

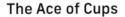

ROOT OF THE
POWERS OF WATER

The Ace of Pentacles

ROOT OF THE
POWERS OF EARTH

The fact that there are no characters pictured in the Aces is clear. The Aces are the seeds of their suit, which will manifest in the remaining cards that follow. Now, it is unrealized potential. The hand holding the symbol of its suit is sometimes called the "Hand of God," or divine intervention. To find a theatrical equivalent, we may look at the Deus Ex Machina, literally "God from the machine." A definition from the Oxford Languages Dictionary defines it by stating that it is "an unexpected power or event saving a seemingly hopeless situation, especially as a contrived plot device in a play or novel."

In the ancient Greek theater, it was a stage machine to bring the gods or heroes of a tragedy onto the stage, usually from a contraption descending from above the stage. Its purpose was to bring the plot to a resolution from a seemingly insoluble crisis.

CARDS WITH MULTIPLE CHARACTERS ON A LEVEL STAGE

The Three of Cups

THE LORD OF ABUNDANCE

We find three women on the same level in some sort of shared celebration. They appear to be dancing among colorful pumpkin patches. None of them "takes the stage," giving one greater status over the other two. The mood of the scene is light; it is set against a light-blue backdrop, and warm colors are used throughout: yellows, oranges, reds, and verdant greens. As noted in the introduction, Katz and Goodwin tell us that these three figures are believed to be Ellen Terry; her daughter, Edy Terry; and Pamela Colman Smith herself. Color coding in the costumes would suggest a relationship between the two US women: they both are wearing white dresses, though one is wearing a yellow tunic over her white garment, and the third is heavily draped in red. It is interesting to note that the costumes go from no drape to lightly draped to heavily draped. It may suggest a difference in their ages and maturity. The two upstage figures may be Edy Craig and Pamela Colman Smith, while the woman downstage in the red garment would likely be Ellen Terry.

The Five of Wands

THE LORD OF STRIFE

We find five young men here engaging in what appears to be playful combat. They all are on equal footing and "battling it out" on a slightly raked playing field. A stage is often raked downward toward the audience so that the stage floor can be seen more easily. This was employed quite often in outdoor stages in the medieval period, and the traveling players of the Commedia dell'arte. The audiences were usually standing, enabling them to see the stage to better advantage; in modern theater, the stage is usually flat and the audience is raked, so the people in the row behind can see over the heads of those in the row in the front of them.

Though the Golden Dawn title tells us that there is strife among them, the bright costumes—particularly the polka-dotted tunic, silhouetted against a cloudless, light-blue sky—suggest that, for now at least, they're just working off some of the exuberance and boundless energy of youth with their pals. If reversed, it may escalate into something less playful, but not for now.

The Four of Wands

THE LORD OF PERFECTED WORK

This stage card is another of celebration. DS we see a structure that reminds us of a chuppah, which, in the Jewish marriage ceremony, symbolizes the stable and loving home that the couple will share. The garland, a bough of celebratory greenery connecting the wands, looks almost like a "smile" (a nod to Paul Quinn in his book *Tarot for Life*). The backdrop is glowing in bright, sunny yellow. The color coding in the costumes suggests a relationship between the two prominent figures. They are wearing white robes, distinguished by a contrasting colored drape. All about this card is joyous, whether it is a marriage ceremony or any celebration of any job well done.

CHARACTERS IN PRONE POSITIONS

The Four of Swords

The Ten of Swords

THE LORD OF
REST FROM STRIFE

THE LORD
OF RUIN

These are the only two cards in the Waite-Smith Tarot deck where we find the figures in prone positions. Some have speculated that they are dead. There are reasons to believe that they are not.

We know that both Smith and Waite were Christians. When a body is laid out for a Christian wake, other than perhaps a high-ranking member of the clergy, the feet are pointed to the west, the head to the east. It is believed that at the Second Coming, when the dead will rise again, they will see Christ before them. That body placement cannot always be ensured, depending on where the wake takes place, but it is virtually certain that the head of the corpse in the coffin is to the viewer's left. In both these cards, the head is to the right. In the Four of Swords, the figure has his hands in a position of prayer, perhaps praying for renewed strength before continuing his quest. For now, we may conclude that he is merely at rest for a time.

In the Ten of Swords, the figure's DS hand is held in a position that would not be seen in the hand of a corpse. After rigor mortis, the hand relaxes (Kaplan et al. 2018). It has also been said that the Ten of Swords is the only card in the deck that illustrates "the Golden Dawn." The Nine of Swords lends support to this notion. In that card, the background is completely black; here we see a strip of yellow in the sky, almost as though the curtain is rising. There is hope, though the journey of recovery will be a challenging one. As with all Tens in the deck, a cycle has ended, and a new one is about to begin.

CHAPTER THIRTEEN

THE COURT CARDS' CURTAIN CALL

QUEEN of WANDS.

KING of WANDS.

Before we leave the minors, the court cards take their final bows. They are, after all, to the manor born and so enjoy the privilege granted them by their royal titles.

The court cards win hands down when it comes to the difficulty for some to understand them, especially when one is new to reading. Perhaps looking at them for yet another perspective may add more clarity. First, in terms of their various relationships with each other, they are a woman and a man—a wife and a husband, a queen and a king. They are shown here as they appear in an ordered deck, first the queen, then the king. This is a very important distinction when examining their relationship to each other. The suits are shown in what I consider their relative speeds. Wands are the fastest of the suits, and Pentacles, the slowest.

The Queen and King of Wands are young, energetic, and vital monarchs. They rule with equal authority with clearly delineated responsibilities. The King faces his queen in profile, SR, acknowledging her shared role. However, there is no doubt that she knows how to negotiate so that he basks in the limelight that he craves. She sits, facing FF, but acknowledges his presence by inclining respectfully in his direction.

There is a sexual energy on display here as well. At any moment, they may make their way to the boudoir. They are definitely partners in every sense of that word.

By observing their body postures and directions, this Queen may even have a slight edge. She is seen here in a very strong position. Perhaps she manages the keys of the kingdom and is the real power behind the throne, at least in those areas of the domain that interest her.

QUEEN of SWORDS.   KING of SWORDS.

The Queen and King of Swords appear more mature. Here she sits in profile, and he full front. She defers to him but is equal to him in strength. Though she is in profile, it is profile right, which is also a powerful position onstage. She has her eyes on the King and the future. Her razor-sharp eyes and her rigid hold of her sword ensure us that she is more than ready to assume the duties of her consort.

While hc is very much in the moment, he is not the visionary that his queen is here. Yet, both can be counted on to mete out fair justice. There is a coolness in the color palette as well, unlike the warmth we noticed in the Queen and King of Wands. Their connection with each other is more ceremonial and is defined by the duties of their royal titles, rather than their vows of marriage.

QUEEN of CUPS.   KING of CUPS.

The Queen and King of Cups appear to be in worlds of their own. This Queen is paying less attention to her royal duties, reducing them to just the necessities of her appointed station. Here she sits with her back to the King, while indulging her unique personal interests. As she faces SR, she may be reminiscing about the life that might have been, and wishes she could turn back the clock, but she is committed to her station in life and must find her escape in her dreams and imaginings. The King, on the other hand, faces us FF. He is duty bound and can be counted on to fulfill his royal obligations, but he might rather abdicate. He is perhaps the king who would be man. Power was never his seductress.

QUEEN of PENTACLES.   KING of PENTACLES.

Finally, with the Queen and King of Pentacles, we immediately observe a similarity in the physical juxtapositions of the previous queen and her consort. In both couples, we see the queens sitting facing SR with their backs to the kings. However, warmth is seen again in this royal pair.

They are older; their flames are not burning so brightly, but they are still very much a devoted couple. They are nearing retirement now and are settled into more-individual preoccupations; since the Queen faces SR, which would suggest the past, she may be thinking of her family, while the King sits FF, satisfied that he has been a good provider, and proud of his accomplishments as a father and as a leader, but the glowing embers of their love are still there.

In summary, of our eight monarchs, the Wands appear to work more compatibly and rule equally and with mutual respect. They consult with each other when making decisions. We can clearly see a strong connection at work here. The King of Swords, Cups, and Pentacles face us FF. They are powerful and effective in their roles, but they work better alone. The Queen of Swords supports the King, though at times she may be seen as the power behind the throne. The other two queens, Cups and Pentacles, have their back to their kings. They seem satisfied with their consorts taking full responsibility of ruling over the kingdom. They are content in their titular roles, which allow them to follow their interests elsewhere.

Exercise

Reverse the positions of each royal couple: first the king, then the queen. How does this change the dynamic of their relationship? Explain the difference in this new arrangement. Do they become closer? Farther apart? Does one gain more power? Lose power?

Write a paragraph in your journal or notebook discussing how different physical juxtapositions may have an impact on the dynamic of their interactions with each other.

This exercise may be applied to any other two cards in the deck when examining the relationship between them, in whatever light you may wish to cast them.

CHAPTER FOURTEEN

A BRIEF WORD ABOUT
THE MAJORS

Though the focus here has been on the Minors, I will touch briefly on the Majors in the Waite-Smith deck. Even though Smith was working under more constraints when designing these cards, the rules and traditions of theatrical staging still pertain. As was referenced earlier, many of the Majors look as though they are posing for their portraits, but there are other implications to those posturings. Though the Majors are not active forces in the themes that are put forth in this book, they may be included in spreads in order to add greater depths of meaning. Mary K. Greer, world-renowned Tarot scholar and author, shared this with me: "Majors are more likely to make pronouncements and speeches rather than develop the plot."

Or, you may think of it this way: Minors are to Majors as questions are to answers. In some cases, a Minor may express a need, and a Major may provide the power and insight to address it. To better understand and grasp the meaning of an individual card, it is essential to work with the cards together, rather than in isolation.

All the Majors that are facing FF represent power, authority, and control of one kind of another (e.g., the Magician, the Emperor, the High Priestess, the Hierophant, Justice, Temperance, the Angels in the Lovers and Judgement, the Hanged Man, the Devil, the Chariot). All the other cards, with human figures, save for the Empress, Death, and the Tower are facing SR from whence they came. As archetypes, those facing SR have traveled great distances in their spiritual quests; they may be reflecting on the lessons learned in their respective karmic journeys, or perhaps they are in a state of receptivity for those who come to them for strength, guidance, and hope. The Hermit is a perfect example. He has reached the summit of his spiritual quest and looks to his right to those who follow him and seek him for enlightenment. Death is the only card in the Majors that is entering SR. He is the mover and the shaker who insists on change for further growth. He travels steadfastly into the future.

Exercise

Turn over cards until you come to the first Minor, and place it upright in front of you. Continue turning cards until you come to the first Major, and place it next to the Minor. Discover what dynamic force is in play when these two entities act and interact with each other.

For example, what advice would the Magician have to offer the passive Four of Cups? Engage them in dialogue. Activate the dialogue in the framework of a spread. The Four of Cups asks the Magician,

1. How do I know what I want?
2. What do I stand to gain? What do I risk losing?
3. What am I willing to sacrifice?
4. What do I need to do? How will I need to do it?
5. What may I expect as a result?

How will the Magician answer each of these questions? And how will the youth in the Four of Cups respond?

Shuffle the entire deck, leaving the Four of Cups and the Magician at the top of the spread as your two main characters. Shuffle and choose one card for each question. Create a horizontal spread. After you've laid down the spread, write a dialogue between the Four of Cups and the Magician. Give them real names and establish their relationship. Raise the stakes in the conflict. That is to say, there is a great deal to be gained, or a great deal can be lost as a result of the outcome of the decisions made. Include the blocking (stage movement). Their body language, their posture, why they move, how they move, and the direction of their movements, arm and hand gestures, facial expressions, and spatial relationships to each other will tell much of the story. The emphasis in this exercise is on the physical lives of these characters and their interactions with each other. These are the kinds of conflicts that Tarot loves to sink her teeth into. She does not react well to trivia.

Sketches from the Majors' Portrait Gallery with Esoteric Functions* from the Golden Dawn

Card meanings adapted from *Bringing the Tarot to Life: Embody the Cards through Creative Exploration*, along with thought-provoking queries to contemplate for each card. The asterisk (*) indicates the esoteric function of each card.

The Fool

THE FOOL.

*NONE

The Fool poses in a dance-like position. There is grace and delicacy in his manner. Notice the way he holds his hands in an air of refinement. This androgynous soul, head held high, is about to take his first spontaneous step into the precipice of the unknown. Regardless, he appears undaunted to whatever may await him. He faces SR. His gaze is focused upward in a kind of innocent, idyllic pose of optimism and wonderment. On his journey of return, he may consider the possible consequences of his decisions and the resources at his disposal before determining that next step—a sign of growth.

What decision-making processes do you consider before making possibly life-changing choices in your life?

David Allen Hulse in *The Western Mysteries* also weighs in on the significance of direction of characters in the Waite-Smith Majors in this one particular instance:

The direction of the Fool is walking from right to left; this is also a secret Key. If the Fool is placed at the head of the Major Arcana series, and the 22 cards are arranged successively, starting with the Fool from right to left (imitating the Hebrew Alphabet), it will be seen that the Fool imitates the cycle of 22 pictures and walks left in the series of cards, while the dancer in the World (Key XXI) is stationed at the end of the series and turns to the right to the receive the energy initiated by the Fool. By this order, Death (Key XIII) is the only other card which walks directly into the Fool. Death being the cessation of our present journey on Earth as the Fool.

A NOTE ABOUT THE LITTLE WHITE DOG

As we know, visual artists, novelists, poets, playwrights, and others use experiences and people from their own lives to inspire story lines and characters.

Pamela Colman Smith was no exception. We know that Smith had a close friendship with the English Victorian actress Ellen Terry and Terry's daughter, Edy Craig; both are cited as likely having inspired a number of characters in the cards she created in the Rider-Waite-Smith Tarot deck.

But what about the little white dog illustrated on the Fool card—the one with the pointed nose and the bushy tail? It is clear to me that it is none other than Ellen Terry's dog, Bruin.

I believe that these pictures of Ellen Terry with her dog bear witness to the inspiration for this iconic little canine who accompanies the Fool on his journey.

The Magician

THE MAGICIAN.

*LIFE AND DEATH

The Magician displays a strong, erect posture in a well-grounded and powerful full-front position. Standing is the strongest of all body postures because it suggests an immediate readiness to move. This powerful energy, when activated by intention, can move mountains. His authority is emphasized by his raised right hand, which is extended even farther by the wand that he holds. "As above, so below."

Where do you need to focus your intention for the highest good?

The High Priestess

THE HIGH PRIESTESS.

*WAR AND PEACE

The High Priestess is FF, sitting quietly and resolute on her throne. This denotes a quality of receptivity, but it is clear that one must come to her for the guidance she may choose to offer. She appears enigmatic and unapproachable. Her mesmerizing stare suggests her inner knowing.

How may activating your own "Inner High Priestess" tap into your deeper, dormant wisdom?

The Empress

THE EMPRESS.

*WISDOM AND FOLLY

The Empress exudes sensuality in every graceful curve of her being. Her throne reflects those lines. Her warm facial expression invites us into her world. The casual way in which she holds her wand tells us that we can relax and be bathed in her loving and nurturing company.

In what ways can you better take care of yourself so that you can share your gift of nurturing to others?

THE EMPEROR.

The Emperor

*SIGHT

The Emperor's character is foursquare in every way. His strong FF position on the throne clearly sends a powerful message of structure and stability. He holds his scepter with a secure grip. His facial expression is stern and unblinking. He does not suffer fools gladly. It's his way or the highway, yet he is fair.

How can you develop these qualities of leadership in your life?

THE HIEROPHANT.

The Hierophant

*HEARING

The Hierophant sits high above us, FF on his throne, which is elevated on a platform. This gives him an even-greater sense of spiritual power and authority based on traditional thinking and theology. He looks above us rather than at us. He is not one of us; he is godlike. Within the boundaries of his theology, he is balanced but does not equivocate when handing down moral advice and judgments.

Which of your traditions comfort you; which ones may be limiting your growth?

THE LOVERS.

The Lovers

*SMELL

The Lovers have nothing to conceal in their nakedness. Both figures gracefully stand FF with arms open and receptive. As he looks to her, and she to the angel, there is a spiritual blending of the earthly and the divine. The angel looks down upon them with arms raised and gives them his blessing. In all, the scene speaks of harmonious balance.

Are there areas of your life that feel out of balance; how can you restore that balance in order to achieve a greater sense of harmony within yourself and with others?

The Chariot

*SPEECH

The charioteer in the Chariot sends a message of power and control. He is standing, looking out FF and elevated by the chariot itself; the chariot also provides a kind of protection. The face of the charioteer conveys a look of determination as he carries on through the obstacles that would impede his journey. The theatrical aspects of this card cannot go unnoticed: the floor of his chariot is a stage, draped with ornate curtains. His esoteric function is "Speech" after all, so it is all of a piece.

How willing are you to work through the challenges that stand between you and achieving your goals? "Per aspera ad astra" ("Through difficulties to the stars").

Strength

*TASTE

Strength reminds us of her powerful gentleness. Her standing figure inclines toward the lion as she looks to him in loving respect. There are no sharp lines in the drawing; all is rendered in graceful curves. Her discipline and control are implicit in her caring demeanor. But is our lower nature, symbolized by the Lion, really tamed? No, it is just under control for the moment. Those who claim power over others do so with the permission of those "controlled" who allow it.

Is there a beast that lives within you that needs taming for your highest good?

The Hermit

*SEXUALITY (TOUCH)

The Hermit has arrived at his destination and is standing, facing SR in a posture of welcome receptivity to those who will follow. His body is strong and erect, his head gently bowed in humility for the gifts he has been given to bestow to those who will receive them. The props he holds in his hands, the staff and the lantern, remind us of the good shepherd.

When have you been the teacher? The student? Which was more rewarding?

Wheel of Fortune

*RICHES AND POVERTY

The Wheel appears to be moving counterclockwise. Looking at it in blocking terms, we see the devil and the snake attached to the wheel from SR, a strong entrance and movement onstage. At first glance the Wheel appears balanced. We also know that a wheel, by its very nature, is going to continue to turn, and its direction will change as well. Our best hope is that, as it spins, it will move in an upward spiral. (I was inspired to visualize the Wheel in this way by Rachel Pollack's illustration of The Spiral of Fortune in her *Shining Tribe Tarot* deck). The air may be more rarified as we ascend, but the view is spectacular!

How can you slow down the wheel so that you don't miss a powerful lesson along the journey?

JUSTICE.

Justice

*WORK

Justice, as we've seen others before her, such as the High Priestess, the Emperor, and the Hierophant, sits on a throne, elevated on a platform in a FF posture with a crown on her head. All of this denotes power and authority; for Justice, the power is legal. Her rulings are balanced and fair. We see that in the sword she balances straight up in her right hand and the balanced scales in her left. The fact that she is not blind-folded tells us that she sees clearly what is brought before her.

What prompts you to act on or ignore an injustice when you see it playing out in front of you?

THE HANGED MAN.

The Hanged Man

*NONE

The Hanged Man has an expression of contentment on his illuminated face. Though he is hanging upside down by one ankle, there appears to be no physical tension in his body. He is there by choice. We cannot see if his hands are restrained behind his back, but we can imagine that they are not. He will know when it is time to leave this state of suspended anima-tion and let himself down. For now, inner spiritual growth trumps interacting with the outside world. The key word here is retreat.

Do you know how to take a time-out when it is needed to refresh the Hanged Man who lives within the soul of your being?

Death

*MOVEMENT

Death is on the move. He is the only one of the Majors who is entering from SR, the strongest of all entrances onstage; he is moving steadfastly into the future (the Sun is somewhat reminiscent of this movement and direction, but he is entering from USC and crossing DSL). Death is separated from the earthly plane by sitting high and erect on his mount. He does not stare in sharp profile R, audience right. There is no need. His destination is predetermined. He appears to be looking out to assure us that change is coming.

Are you living in a chapter of your life that is out of date? Is it time to move out of the rut that is stunting your growth, and move into a new and invigorating life experience?

DEATH.

Temperance

*ANGER

Temperance exudes physical and spiritual balance as he carefully pours the energies of life from one chalice to the other. His face is relaxed; he pours with assuredness. The entire motif of the illustration is one of balance: the wings, the crown, and the irises; the road and the rocks; and the chalices themselves, both held with a loose but steady grip.

How have you achieved balance in your life? When it is imbalanced, what resources do you call upon to make it right again?

TEMPERANCE.

The Devil

*LAUGHTER

The Devil's hypnotic glare, with right hand raised, pledges to us that he is in charge of our lower nature. His splayed legs are precariously balanced on a too-small cube. His place in our psyche is not guaranteed. The Devil's minions are reminiscent of the Lovers, still naked but now chained. There is

THE DEVIL.

no divine connection here as we saw with the Lovers. They appear oblivious to a divine presence as they cast their gaze to the dark earth below them. Their consciousness is still in reach of liberation from the Devil's grip.

What are you willing to let go of in your life that does not serve you? What would you put in its place to rise to your highest good?

The Tower

THE TOWER.

*INDIGNATION AND GRACE

The Tower assures us that the walls will come tumbling down, eventually, in order to awaken us to an ego that has become too self-satisfied and complacent for further growth. The very ground must open and swallow us up before we can experience a reawakening. The falling figures, still alive and free of the flames, provide some optimism that they will survive the fall and experience a rebirth. Amid all the fire and chaos, the Tower remains virtually white, showing no signs of crumbling to the ground. It remains standing as a beacon of hope that not all is lost.

What did it take to jar you into the greatest revelation of your life? How did it change your trajectory?

The Star

THE STAR.

*IMAGINATION

The Star may be the most welcoming card in the majors. Her naked and open body reveals graceful, soft curves, with nothing to hide. She kneels facing SR. She has arrived here from her long journey and is now ready, literally, with outstretched arms, to welcome us in as we meet her on our life's path. After the fall from grace from Death and the Tower, she provides hope and well-being for a better future. She is reminiscent of Temperance; once the energies are balanced, she pours them unstintingly onto the parched earth so that we may soak them up and revive.

How can you activate a process now that will lead toward fulfilling your long-awaited wish? "Hope sees the invisible; feels the intangible; achieves the impossible." —Helen Keller

The Moon

*SLEEP

The Moon looks down on us with an air of cool serenity, giving little away yet bathing us in its cool light and soothing our lower instincts. The way forward is not without obstacles to surmount, but the gates are open wide, and the way is clearly in view by the reflection of the moon's gentle illumination.

What is hiding in the shadows of your life right now that would benefit from exposure to the light? What can you do to clear the way?

The Sun

*FERTILITY AND BARRENNESS

The Sun allows no room for ambiguity here. She smiles down on us with warm, life-assuring radiance; the sky is blue; the garden is flourishing; the innocent child is naked, trusting, and unafraid as he rides DSL, arms and legs untethered by saddle or bridle. The boy even dons the quirky feather of the Fool, assuring us that the Fool has made it this far and is still very much alive in the free spirit of the child.

How has shining a bright light on the road ahead assisted you in making decisions that have enriched the quality of your life?

JUDGEMENT.

Judgement

*NONE

Judgement assigns the Angel Gabriel to blow his clarion trumpet, calling those who have surrendered their old ways to a more fulfilling life. Those gray, ghostly bodies with wide-open arms are answering the call. Balance is restored once more. We see it in the symmetry of the welcoming spread of Gabriel's wings, the equilateral cross, the two balanced groups of three bodies emerging from their coffins. Life's red blood will soon be flowing through their veins once more.

Is there a calling that you are ignoring and hoping it will go away? If so, what impact is that having on the quality of your life now?

THE WORLD.

The World

*POWER AND SERVITUDE

And all's right with the World. She has found her bliss. Again, we find her naked, free, and open. She looks back over her SR shoulder, taking stock of her journey, and says, "Well done!" She has come full circle. She has been awarded a wand by the Magician, and for reaching her karmic destiny, she has been given another!

Exercise

If you can truly say, "All's right with the world," what did it take to make it so? If it is not, what will be required? This will include everything that you can do and what the world at large can do. Make two columns and list five examples for each.

What can I do?

1._____

2._____

3._____

4._____

5._____

What must nations do around the globe?

1._____

2._____

3._____

4._____

5._____

CHAPTER FIFTEEN

SPREADS

Directions

As you lay out your cards in the following spreads, pay particular attention to the direction the cards are facing. Are they passive or active? If there is implied movement, is it SL or SR, US or DS? Is the character elevated or on a flat surface? What insights can you gain from these observations?

Observe the body language: Standing or sitting? Erect? Stooped? Or prone?

If the cards are interacting with each other, are they facing each other or do they seem to be moving away from each other?

How can these insights bring another depth of understanding to your readings?

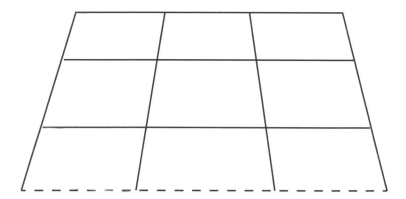

A Second "Staged Reading" Spread

These are the nine acting blocks on a stage (see the diagram in chapter 2). We discussed in chapter 2 the relative strength of each area and the power it holds. Below are nine questions. Place each question in a block that seems most appropriate. Lay out nine cards in a pattern, following the diagram above.

You may also wish to make up your own questions.

1. Where am I now?
2. Where do I aspire to be?
3. How am I to my detriment?
4. How am I to my betterment?
5. Who or what is the obstacle holding me back?
6. How do I currently respond to the obstacle?
7. What is the best course of action right now?
8. Where may I look for support?
9. What is the possible outcome?

Example for number 5: Perhaps someone is a negatively powerful influence in your life. You might write that question in the DSC block. This is a very powerful position. In general, DS is stronger than US. SR is stronger than SL. Higher is stronger than lower. Now shuffle your deck and lay one card at a time facedown on the block of your choice. You may want to use two of these graphs, so you can keep track of where you wrote the questions. Now turn one card over at a time and interpret the message. Notice how the cards acknowledge and interact with each other. You may wish to move the cards around like chess pieces to see how that might change the dynamics. Play with it. There are endless outcomes and possibilities. Pay close attention to direction in each card and, on that basis, observe how the cards are interacting with each other.

You may also wish to lay out nine cards and read them as a "French scene"* in which several characters are interacting; include in your interpretation their names, relationship, conflict, resolution, dialogue, and blocking.

*"French scene": The introduction and resolution of a minor conflict in the larger context of the play

Exercise

Write the dialogue for this scene, including the stage directions, in your journal or notebook.

The Upstaging Spread

"Upstaging" is gaining status or power over another character. How does that play out in your personal life?

- A. Who or what upstages you?
- B. How is it done?
- C. How do you allow it?
- D. How can you oppose it?
- E. What is the likely outcome?

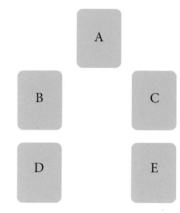

Directions

Lay out your cards one at a time, beginning with A. Write a short paragraph about the insights and conclusions you may have drawn from this spread.

A: _____

B: _____

C: _____

D: _____

E: _____

Relationship Spread # 1*

A relationship spread is a good way to focus on the topics covered in this book. Pay close attention to direction and body language. This spread directs your attention to

- where the person/couple is in the relationship (status). (This can be any kind of a relationship. Ignore gender unless you find it relevant to your reading.)
- the need/want that motivates or drives participants to maintain or dissolve the relationship.
- possibilities for the relationship—the perspective of each person is considered in each of the three areas.

There are six cards in all, laid out in three rows of two cards each and read as follows:

First row: Relationship focus/intentions
(Card 1 and Card 2) or
(Person 1 and Person 2, respectively)
Cards 3 and 5 are aspects of Person 1.
Cards 4 and 6 are aspects of Person Two.

1.  2.

Second row: Relationship needs/desires
(Card 3 and Card 4)

3.  4.

Third row: Potential outcome/future
(Card 5 and Card 6)

5.  6.

Relationship Spread # 2*

Example of a Relationship Happiness spread (said to be inspired by Gandhi).

Before reading the directions below, look at each pair of cards and imagine the dynamic that may exist between them, were they in a relationship.

1. A & B: What are you and your partner thinking about each other? (unspoken)

2. A & B: What are you and your partner saying to each other? (how you communicate)

3. A & B: What are you and your partner doing to each other? (how you treat each other)

4. A & B: Advice on how to create more harmony between what you think, say, and do)

5. Current happiness potential. Turn over an additional card under each of the four pairs to reveal the current happiness potential between each set.

Be the change you want to see in your relationship!

Instructions: Practice with the spread above, then shuffle the deck and, using the same spread, lay out one of your own.

Note their physical proximity to each other:

> Are they blending?

> Are they separating?

> Are they moving closer?

> Is their body language receptive? Closed off?

> What level of energy is detected in their body posture? Excitement? Boredom? Fear? Hesitancy? Anticipation? Etc.

NOTES

_____

_____

_____

_____

_____

Exercise

"CASTING DIRECTOR"

Choose a play, movie, or television drama with a wide variety of characters. In column 1 that follows, list the names of the characters (five, or more if you like).

In column 2, choose a Tarot card that best suits each character. Explain.

In column 3, list two or three character/personality traits they share in common. (You may want to do this on a separate piece of paper if you find you need more space.)

Column 1   Column 2   Column 3

1._____   _____   _____

2._____   _____   _____

3._____   _____   _____

4._____   _____   _____

5._____   _____   _____

THE JUDGEMENT SPREAD

Each of the seventy-eight cards in a Tarot deck is active in all of us at one time or another. At various junctures, one card appears more active than another, and then that is what we notice as it manifests in behavior.

Let's say that all the cards are "Houses"; the House of Strength, for example. Within the house, there are "Rooms." In one of the rooms in the House of Strength is Higher Nature; in another, Control, while in still another, Inner Strength, or Courage.

For this exercise, we will look at the Judgement card as the "House" and then look into each "Room" of the house to see what resides there. Each room will ask the visitor four questions. These questions compose the spread for each room.

Lay out four cards in a horizontal row for each reading, with the Judgement card placed above them.

This can be done for every card in the deck. For example, there may be a House of the Eight of Swords, the House of the Page of Wands, or the House of the Devil.

Again, focus on directions and levels you see in the spread, and interactions between and among characters, and integrate those observations in your readings. You may wish to add the Judgement card back into the deck to see if it may appear again in one of the "House" readings. This will draw special attention to that spread of four questions.

In this example,
the Judgement card has
been selected:

The House of Judgement
True Calling

1. What is your true calling?
2. How have you answered it?
3. How have you denied it?
4. What has been the result?

Starting Over

1. In what area of your life would you like to start over?
2. What might you gain?
3. What might you lose?
4. What first step could you take now?

The Paralysis of Past Experience

1. What old ways of thinking and behaving do you need to go beyond
   in order to move forward?
2. How have these ways stunted your growth?
3. How have they affected those around you?
4. How may you experience a new awakening by adopting new
   ways of thinking and behaving?

Resurrection of Self

1. What good has died within you?
2. How can you resurrect it?
3. What would renewal look like?
4. What chain of events might it set in motion?

Neglect

1. What area of your life have you neglected?
2. How has it affected you?
3. How has it affected others?
4. What do you need to do to change that for the better?

Bad Judgment

1. In what area of your life have you recently made a bad judgment?
2. What were the consequences?
3. At this point, how can you attempt to remedy the current outcome?
4. What benefit may be derived?

Crossroads

1. In what crossroad of life do you find yourself?
2. What would need to happen before you could move in one direction or another?
3. What risk might you need to take to facilitate this move?
4. In what new direction is it likely to take you?

Growing Pains

1. What hard lesson may be left for you to learn?
2. Who or what may be your teacher?
3. What sacrifice may be asked of you?
4. What new insights may await?

A New Life

1. What brought you to where you are now?
2. Where are you headed?
3. How will you get there?
4. What will you find?

A Life-Changing Event (A Wake-Up Call)

1. What did you learn about yourself?
2. What did you learn about others?
3. How did you resist the change?
4. In what ways did you rise to a more meaningful life?

CHAPTER SIXTEEN

CONCLUSION

So why was Smith's contribution to this iconic Tarot deck largely taken for granted until rather recently? Even from its inception, her work was undervalued. Referring to her commission for designing the deck, Smith is quoted as saying, "I received very little cash for a big job" (Kaplan et al. 2018).

Curiously enough, when people are asked about their favorite Tarot deck, they will often say, "Rider-Waite." Rider was the publisher of the deck, "Rider & Company." It wasn't until 2009, when the centennial edition of the deck was published, that one began hearing the Rider-Waite-Smith deck or simply Waite-Smith. Of course, loyalists from the beginning surely acknowledged Smith's role in designing this deck. But in 2009, it reached the mainstream. The modern Tarot community must be credited as well for correcting this long injustice and bringing to light Pamela Colman Smith's rightful place of honor in the world of Tarot.

For the lion's share of that credit, we turn to the late Stuart R. Kaplan, founder of U.S. Games Inc., who lifted her name from the dusty vaults of Tarot history and into the glow of celebrity status that she so rightly deserved.

Just eight years later, in 2017, the Me Too movement began, which put a point on the contributions that women have made to our culture and in all areas of our lives. No doubt, Miss Smith would have been at the forefront of that movement were she alive today.

In the same year that her iconic deck was published, she was also very active in the right-to-vote movement as well as in Suffrage Atelier, an organization that in part prepared for a demonstration by the Women's Social and Political Union, uniting with other organizations to support the work of artists and actresses (Kaplan et al. 2018).

Smith's influence in the Tarot community is more evident now that ever. Her iconic deck has captured the imaginations of thousands who followed her with their clone decks of the Waite-Smith original. New decks are coming out, virtually on a daily basis. I alone have shelves and drawers filled with them as proof of that.

The experience in writing this book was an interesting and challenging one. My

intention was to propose how Smith's theater background informed her illustrations of these cards and their meanings. I attempted to set aside what I know about the cards, and concentrate on them as still frames from a play. The final product morphed into a blending of the two. What I have suggested in this book concerning the physical lives of these cards is purely educated speculation on my part. But there is no doubt that Pamela Colman Smith's theatrical background, in part, informed her wonderfully imaginative depictions on these seventy-eight iconic cards. I hope the approach I have taken has added something worthwhile to the conversation and provided another tool to glean further meanings from the Rider Waite Smith Tarot Deck.

CHAPTER SEVENTEEN

THE MINORS

Traditional Tarot card meanings along with their astrological attributions (Ace through Ten) of the Minor Suits (Wands, Swords, Cups, Pentacles)

(Adapted and revised from my book *Bringing the Tarot to Life: Embody the Cards through Creative Exploration*)

Ace of Wands

THE ROOT OF THE POWERS OF FIRE

The Ace of Wands heralds new beginnings. It is the fire of enthusiasm, inspiration, and strong desire. It is the vital spark needed to take risks and launch new projects. It is bursting with energy, particularly sexual energy. This is a card that says, "Go; now is the time to seize the day!"

If you ignore its insistence, then energy and creativity are blocked; your interest fizzles, or you may attempt half-hearted efforts that fail. Your sexuality may be out of control, or you may feel impotent as a result of a weak libido.

Two of Wands

MARS IN AIRES

The Two of Wands is about where one is, or perhaps where one once was, vs. where he wants to be, and asking himself: "Is this all there is?" It is a time of feeling successful but bored, having everything and wanting more. This would be a good time to consider a profitable partnership or to ponder over the next step. This may require choosing between security and adventure. Being overly cautious or lacking in motivation and ambition may be the stumbling block.

On the contrary, you may stop procrastinating and take the risk to regain that sense of competing in the unpredictable but exciting arena of life. You may take on a new role or launch a new and challenging enterprise.

Three of Wands

SUN IN ARIES

The Three of Wands is centered and focused on the future. It is wait and see after the bread has been cast upon the water. As a result of purposeful living, you are on the right track, and your ideas have taken off. You may have broadened your horizons through group cooperation and teamwork.

Though this is a period of resting strength, don't wait too long or you may miss the boat. A project could fail as a result of fearing to venture out. The initial project is complete, but there is room for expansion. The work is not finished.

Four of Wands

VENUS IN ARIES

This is a time of peace and harmony, security, renewal of life, a celebration after a period of hard work. It is that healthy balance between work and play. Relationships blossom; a proposal of marriage is in the air. This is also a rite of passage, which could include graduations, buying a new house, retirement, or coming out.

All is going well, even when happiness may not be so obvious: the celebration may have been somewhat disappointing, or you may be afraid to join the "free-spirited" group but wish you could. Keep in mind that "all work and no play makes Jack a dull boy!"

Five of Wands

SATURN IN LEO

There is conflict here, but it is more about competing for the sheer joy of it. It is that adrenaline rush that comes when the wands are on fire. There is fighting, but no one gets harmed. There is rivalry; there are arguments and disagreements. But rules are honored. It all takes place in the context of good fun and fair play.

There are exceptions though. Sometimes the rules are thrown out and the fighting becomes ugly; the competition is unhealthful. When rules are ignored, expect to see unethical behavior, one-upmanship, and sore losers.

Six of Wands

JUPITER IN LEO

This is pure and unadulterated victory. You have reached the top of your game as a charismatic leader. You are now receiving all the recognition and high praise that you deserve. You are enjoying a hero's welcome from your enthusiastic followers, who shower you with accolades and awards.

If victory goes to your head, however, you may quickly find yourself a legend in your own mind. Beware of vanity, hogging all the credit, or becoming a user. Resting on your laurels may lead to a rudely awakening defeat and a loss of power.

Seven of Wands

MARS IN LEO

When you are uncertain of victory, it is time to stand your ground. At the same time, keep in mind that you are on a slippery slope of control and need to know when to retreat. The competition is unhealthful here, and you may find yourself struggling to survive.

Conversely, you may be overreacting to a perceived adversary. Do not reject support if it is offered, or be blind to the opportunity for diplomacy. Here the project may have been aborted, or you may be on the road to undermining your ultimate goal.

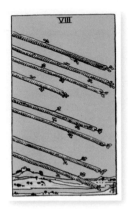

Eight of Wands

MERCURY IN SAGITTARIUS

The Eight of Wands points to everything going in the right direction. It may be a group of people working positively and harmoniously toward a shared goal. It may be a literal journey, possibly by air, or action taken in a love affair. You may be swept off your feet and enjoying the rush. No wonder, then, that this card is sometimes called "the Arrows of Love." It may also indicate finding direction in life and moving toward greater clarity. Whatever it is, it is happening swiftly.

If you miss the target, though, everything may seem up in the air. You may be getting ahead of yourself or looking for a quick fix when more-methodical planning is called for. Sometimes speed sacrifices quality.

Nine of Wands

MOON IN SAGITTARIUS

If you see life as perpetual conflict, then you are always poised for a fight. That chip on your shoulder may have been brought on by past wounds. However, you can feel drained from feeling you must always be on guard. You may be holding on to childhood survival strategies long after they are necessary or useful. If so, they may be getting in the way of current growth and maturity.

Accept a helping a hand if it is offered, and let go of your conviction of righteousness. This is not to say that you should let down your guard altogether. It is important to remain vigilant and cautious when the threat is real.

Ten of Wands

SATURN IN SAGITTARIUS

There are those who are in love with responsibility. They complain, but they wouldn't have it any other way. They are the classic workaholics, the martyrs whose motto is "Do it all or it won't be done 'right.'"

The downside of the workhorse, however, is feeling oppressed and burdened by life. There's no denying that the job gets done, but at what price? Now may be the time to get in touch with your limitations and learn to delegate. You may discover a new lease on life when you allow time for yourself. Remember, cemeteries are filled with people who thought they were indispensable.

Page of Wands

PAGE of WANDS.

The Page of Wands is the youthful student or one who is young in spirit. He may also mark a new phase in life or the start of a project or relationship. He is the innocent opportunist with the attitude of "Look out, world; here I come!" He is ambitious and idealistic and has an active imagination, willing to take creative risks, which are inspired by his fiery passion. He is precocious and simply enjoys life just for itself with no external pressure. He may lack social graces, but he has a kind of quirkiness that is appealing. He has a strong and healthy sex drive.

He can be stymied by disruptions when life does not meet his expectations. Then, he can become confused and indecisive and lose his self-confidence. He can become the hyperactive and unmanageable child, who acts irresponsibly and impulsively. Not having a creative outlet can lead to depression and isolation, or he may try to compensate by burning the candle at both ends.

Knight of Wands

KNIGHT of WANDS.

The Knight of Wands is a type A personality, a real show-off but good natured in his boasting and action-driven life. He is an idealist who lives by inspiration. He is apt to fly off in all directions, so he needs something to focus on to channel his irrepressible energy. He loves change, so that is why is he is drawn to travel, adventure, and secret missions. He has an irresistible urge to "go for it." He has a generous spirit and is devoted to his friends, although he may infuriate them at times. Though he is the object of many erotic fantasies, he is not ready to settle down. He's a "Love 'em and leave 'em" kind of guy.

He needs to be careful that his hot head does not get the better of him. He can become a braggart and a bully—a rebel without a cause. He is easily thrown when he is not grounded, and his fire gives way to depression. He can demand recognition when he does not get his way.

Queen of Wands

QUEEN of WANDS.

The Queen of Wands is warm and compassionate. People are drawn to her. When she enters a room, it becomes electric. She is vibrant and powerful in her role as a charismatic leader. She is a walking cornucopia of ideas and is tirelessly busy. She radiates love and a certain joie de vivre. She has a seemingly charmed life and cordially gets her way. She is a terrific hostess and a great friend. She can be rather theatrical, but that is part of her charm. She is also bold and the most sexual of the queens.

She struggles with setbacks, however, and when she sees life as unfair, she can become bitter. Under those circumstances, she can display her controlling and aggressive nature: "It's my way or the highway!" She can become temperamental, even ferocious, when attacked or when defending others. Her good nature depends on life responding in a positive way. When her generosity is not received with what she considers appropriate appreciation, she may become judgmental and resentful.

King of Wands

KING of WANDS.

The King of Wands is a natural-born leader and is at the top of his game. He is positive, optimistic, truthful, and intolerant of weakness: "If I can do it, so can you." He is charismatic, self-assured, charming, and a great communicator—a real take-charge kind of guy. He can be an entrepreneur, a philanthropist, a business leader, or a politician. He has powerful drive and strong sex appeal.

The downside here can be a loss of identity without his accustomed role. Melancholy may set in, or he may become a self-centered despot who is hot tempered, uncompromising, and impulsive. This behavior earns him the crown of "King Baby."

Ace of Swords

ACE of SWORDS.

THE ROOT OF THE POWER OF AIR

With the Ace of Swords comes the gift of intellect, pure perception, and clarity. It signals the birth of a bright idea. Associated with law and order, it insists on truth above all as it impartially weighs both sides of an issue. The sword cuts through material reality to reach the pure mind. In a literal sense, it can also predict that surgery will be successful.

However, when the sword isn't there to serve the highest good, it can indicate that your power was used badly, that your ideas are confused, and that you are procrastinating with indecisiveness. In everyday parlance, it may suggest unsuccessful surgery, writer's block, or . . . the condom broke!

Two of Swords

MOON IN LIBRA

The Two of Swords speaks of going inward in order to keep the world at bay. What weighs in the balance may concern a decision that needs to be made between desire and duty. Are you putting up barriers against someone who is trying to help you? It may be a time to go on a retreat for meditation and soul-searching.

The result of this kind of introspection may be a renewed commitment to restore balance and move past mental blocks to become more open to compromise. You may begin by removing divisions between yourself and others.

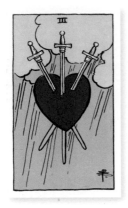

Three of Swords

SATURN IN LIBRA

With the Three of Swords, the mind has lacerated the heart, bringing with it mental anguish, heartbreak, and suffering. You may be torturing yourself mentally over a complicated relationship, a betrayal, or a failed affair. Then again, it may be you who is bringing sorrow to someone else.

In rare cases, the Three of Swords may predict the possibility of a heart attack. If that is the case, this will serve as a reminder to make better decisions concerning your health. More optimistically, if heart surgery is indicated, this card bodes well for its success. The mental process of healing will begin with facing the problem head on and allowing the healing process to begin. Procrastination can exacerbate the pain and make it feel overwhelming.

Four of Swords

JUPITER IN LIBRA

The Four of Swords is a time of withdrawal for the purpose of meditation, and healing—physical, mental, or spiritual. It may also be a needed break from the ordinary worries of the day. To that end, an escape from the rat race by taking a holiday or a spiritual pilgrimage for restoration and rejuvenation may be recommended. Then again, it may indicate sleep, where solutions to your problems are revealed in dreams.

Finally, the card warns of staying too long in the comfort zone; this may lead to worry, stagnation, and boredom. Eventually, it is necessary to return to active life with a renewed commitment to live your life more productively.

Five of Swords

VENUS IN AQUARIUS

There is more than enough defeat, humiliation, and shame to go around in the Five of Swords. There are winners who will win at any cost, but "at what price, glory?" We see a Pyrrhic victory for one who has won the battle but lost the war. The victory was won dubiously by abuse, cheating, and bullying.

If you are the one defeated, it is important to avoid letting your defeat define you or mourning over losing a battle or a stupid fight. Cut your losses and move on. If there is any consolation, the victory over you may be short lived.

Six of Swords

MERCURY IN AQUARIUS

The Six of Swords speaks of a passage to greater understanding. It might involve a physical journey, but more likely a spiritual one. It is certainly a passage toward peace after making a difficult decision. Though the going is rough, better times are coming. Support has been offered and you have wisely accepted. You have learned what to leave behind in order to concentrate on growth and to seek a safer harbor.

If, on the contrary, you are so paralyzed by conflict that you see no foreseeable way out, you may become a victim of your own indecisiveness. You may think your friends are "jumping ship" and leaving you behind.

Seven of Swords

MOON IN AQUARIUS

The Seven of Swords is often seen as one who is crafty with hidden agendas. You may see him as someone who is two-faced, sneaky, a thief, a con artist, a liar, or a spy. He tiptoes around issues to avoid facing them directly. He acts spontaneously and impulsively when careful planning is required.

If that's not the case, then he may be a clever diplomat who understands the need for secrecy. He may even be taking back what is rightfully his or returning stolen goods. At times, this card suggests elopement or a secret affair.

Eight of Swords

JUPITER IN GEMINI

The Eight of Swords is about living within perceived boundaries. It includes oppression, humiliation, shame, and isolation. You're living in an imaginary prison, believing in your own helplessness. Your problems are self-imposed, perhaps brought on by fear of change. You may also be chained to fixed ideas, or you are intimidated by authority.

A more positive approach is to work on overcoming your fears and building your self-confidence. When you realize that you are the source of your past, you can get out of your own way, admit you're stuck, and seek help.

Nine of Swords

MARS IN GEMINI

When the Nine of Swords surfaces, you may be steeped in deep sorrow, agonizing mental pain, panic attacks, nightmares, insomnia, and the demons you do not want to face. It may also include fear of dying, overwhelming depression, and self-doubt. Feeling there's no way out may put you on the verge of a mental breakdown. The pain suffered by those you love may also be the source of your grief.

Often, things are not as bad as they seem. There is light at the end of the tunnel. Liberation can begin by confronting your pain and fears. This would be a good time to come out of isolation and seek support, whether it is from a friend or a professional therapist.

Ten of Swords

SUN IN GEMINI

The Ten of Swords signifies the end of a downward spiral. New life springs from the clarity that results from facing painful revelations. You've hit rock bottom by thinking things to death and overly exaggerating your plight in life. Your vision of the universe as oppressive, antagonistic, and chaotic may not have been accurate after all.

There are times, though, when the Ten of Swords is as painful as it seems. If that's the case, then backstabbing, disloyalty, psychological breakdown, and even death may not be out of the question. On a lighter note, it may just be time to make an appointment with the acupuncturist or get over being a drama queen.

PAGE of SWORDS.

Page of Swords

The Page of Swords is often seen with his head in the clouds and appearing above it all. He needs lots of mental stimulation to escape being bored. He is witty and intelligent and is proficient with words and writing. He can hold his ground with adults. He is impatient with fools and intolerant of authority, since he is the self-proclaimed "smartest kid in the class." Yes, he can be a precocious brat.

He can also be overly critical, sarcastic, and cynical. If he appears aloof and detached, it may be attributable to his being a loner and socially awkward. He would prefer to be an outside observer rather than the life of the party. He has qualities that would make him a good spy. His suspicious and defensive nature may come from early-childhood betrayal or wounding.

KNIGHT of SWORDS.

Knight of Swords

The Knight of Swords is attracted to causes. He is a fierce competitor, brave, skillful, and ambitious. He is invested in being "right." He likes living in the fast lane. He can be very opinionated, impatient, and headstrong. He may defeat you with a barrage of elevated language. He is a master of "death by words." He is keenly intelligent, loves excellence, and is often more respected than liked. As a lover, he is a "fly by night."

If he fails to channel his mental energies, he can start projects with excitement and end them in chaos. He is not above stealing your ideas and arguing for the sake of arguing. As he ages, he may begin to soften and abandon his cold logic for greater empathy.

Queen of Swords

QUEEN of SWORDS.

The Queen of Swords knows both sorrow and wisdom from hard experience. She faces pain courageously. She uses her intellect to free herself from confusion. She can be very critical and usually sees what's "wrong" first. She has a sharp tongue and can be tactless and sarcastic. In her eyes, dishonesty is punishable by dismissal. She does not suffer fools gladly. She is well educated, and as a problem solver she is just, fair, and truthful. As a parent, she believes in "tough love." She can be loving but always keeps something of herself for herself.

At her best, she is charming and witty, attracting listeners and followers. She is an idealist without illusions. She needs lots of time alone to recharge and regroup. With age, she may begin to soften and show emotion. Her filters may become stronger, so that she will think a little more before she speaks.

King of Swords

KING of SWORDS.

The King of Swords is synonymous with authority, power, judgment, wisdom, and fair-mindedness. He is often a man of law or a counselor who is tough and sometimes rigid, but always objective and impartial. He ignores thinking that depends on preconception and prejudice. He can delegate authority, but his is the final say; his voice is absolute. There's nothing personal when heads need to roll. He has the ability to unveil truth behind appearances. As a partner, he can be dominating and controlling.

If he becomes corrupt, then he abuses his power and uses it for personal gain. He will argue for its own sake in the role of devil's advocate; the letter of the law becomes more important than the spirit of the law. He can become cold, impersonal, and emotionally unavailable. Later in life, his emotional side may manifest.

ACE of CUPS.

Ace of Cups

THE ROOT OF THE POWERS OF WATER

The Ace of Cups embraces emotional happiness, joy and loving, caring relationships, creativity, and heartfelt inspiration. It is truly a gift from the heart. At times, it may also suggest a new relationship, marriage, fertility, conception, and birth—particularly of a girl. Additionally, this Ace may represent kindness, compassion, emotional growth, and trusting your heart and, in the process, learning to love yourself.

If the Ace of Cups is to your detriment, it could point to a fear of commitment, unhappiness, or the end of an affair. You could be feeling new love and passion but hesitating to allow it in. Regarding reproduction, it may indicate infertility or a delay in pregnancy.

Two of Cups

VENUS IN CANCER

The Two of Cups heralds the beginning of a new relationship. It could be romantic in nature but could just as well be discovering your soulmate or a compatible business partner. Like all the Twos, it is about balance, cooperation, and an agreeable union between doing and feeling and the willingness to do what it takes to make it work.

When there is negative energy around the Two of Cups, there may be a failure to communicate, or love is feigned. Furthermore, this card may be saying that you should be mindful of unrealistic expectations in a relationship and to avoid overdependence on a partner.

Three of Cups

MERCURY IN CANCER

The Three of Cups is about finding your own tribe and celebrating with joy and shared experiences. It is a happy event, a party, teamwork and trust among friends, or finding solace with them during a difficult time.

Conversely, the Three of Cups may advise against overdependence on group acceptance. You may feel like you don't belong, or there has been a breakup of a group of friends. It may also point to discord brought on from lack of teamwork. You may be overly indulging in sensual pleasure (e.g., alcoholism, gluttony, sloth); be wary of ménage à trois. It may be time to go on the wagon. On a more mundane level, the party was canceled.

Four of Cups

MOON IN CANCER

The Four of Cups is oblivious to opportunity when it is staring him in the face. This may come from apathy, restlessness, depression, or complacency. There is a sense of sameness that breeds boredom and lifelessness. You may have become too comfortable with the status quo.

On the flip side, you may simply need time for yourself to meditate and to contemplate, so you have intentionally withdrawn in order to find new purpose. You'll know when it's time to "look a gift horse in the mouth." When you come out of yourself, you feel invigorated, ready to take risks and embrace new opportunities.

Five of Cups

MARS IN SCORPIO

The Five of Cups is focused so much of what's lacking that little or no attention is paid to what remains. You may be grieving from some sort of loss; a relationship has ended or you're beating yourself up for what might have been.

When you are able to turn the page, you may leave your isolation and look toward the future with a more realistic view of the past. At this juncture, you are more likely to accept support from others, with a commitment to rebuilding your life and moving forward. If the loss is about the death of a loved one, after grief, there is relief.

Six of Cups

SUN IN SCORPIO

Like all the Sixes, the Six of Cups is about giving and receiving. In this case, it is about the sharing of sweet memories, nostalgia, or serene moments in the present as you reminisce with an old friend. You may also be picturing your childhood as a safe and happy time. In some instances, it is about caring for someone more vulnerable, whether it is a child or an older adult.

From another perspective, you may be clinging to a fixation on the past, unwilling to change, and disappointed in friends who grow up and leave you behind. Ideally, you should let go of the past if it is crippling, live in the present, and look forward to the future.

Seven of Cups

VENUS IN SCORPIO

In the Seven of Cups, you are blessed and cursed with the paralysis of abundance. In trying to weigh your many options, you may become indecisive and overwhelmed by the choices before you. As a result, you may find that you are confused between reality and fantasy. With your head in the clouds, wishful thinking may have replaced purposeful doing.

When greater stability enters the picture, false assumptions are abandoned and dreams are exchanged for reality. There is also the possibility that you were seduced by fantasy, and your dreams are dashed. Cliché, but nonetheless true: "Be careful what you wish for."

Eight of Cups

SATURN IN PISCES

The Eight of Cups professes that it is time to leave a good thing behind and search for something better. Perhaps a doctor with a successful home practice joins Doctors without Borders. It is a difficult decision, but necessary for growth. Perhaps it is seeking greater inner awareness or moving from dogma to your own vision; it could even be knowing when it is time to leave a support group.

If detachment is too threatening to your security, then you may be in danger of hanging on after the cup has run dry. Or perhaps you are being too hasty in your decision to leave. There may be more to reap before you set out to sow on higher ground.

Nine of Cups

JUPITER IN PISCES

"Eat, Drink, and Be Merry!" That's the watch cry of the Nine of Cups. Here, you may be indulging in hedonistic pleasures: feasting, pleasures of the flesh, casual sex (i.e., legs spread, heart blocked), enjoying the good life. In the most healthful sense, you are taking a break from the rigors of life that is needed for refreshment. Everything in moderation—that's the key.

There can be too much of a good thing, and it can lead to addiction and risky behavior. You may be in that phase of substance abuse when you think you're still in control. Now is the time to reach out for support, leave material pleasures behind, and seek a spiritual awakening.

Ten of Cups

MARS IN PISCES

The Ten of Cups epitomizes "the Perfect Family." The heart has found its home and is surrounded by loved ones, life's sweet blessings, simple pleasures, harmony, and tranquility. You are grateful for the riches of life and are sharing it with others.

If the Ten of Cups takes a downward spiral, then perhaps "the Perfect Family" is not so perfect after all. There may be domestic unrest: divorce, rebellious children, or physical damage to your home. At times, this card may also represent alternative families (e.g., same-sex couples, communes, or religious affiliations, such as megachurches or cults).

Page of Cups

PAGE of CUPS.

The Page of Cups is free from responsibility, so he can indulge in fantasy and develop his psychic abilities. He truly is an old soul in a young body. He is sensitive, artistic, creative, joyful, and intuitive. He is the most romantic and sentimental of the pages, and sometimes a rather naive and gullible idealist.

Work is not his forte; he'd rather inspire than perspire. He can be unreliable, given to flights of fancy, broken promises, and shallow commitments, and lying is not a new concept for him—but he means well. In romance, he can become a victim in an emotional relationship if he becomes overly needy for love and reassurance.

Knight of Cups

KNIGHT of CUPS.

The Knight of Cups is a charming dreamer, but not particularly good at completing anything. He is self-indulgent, chases rainbows, and, generally, is bored with the real world. He frustrates those around him as he builds castles in the sky. He's hopelessly romantic but often a heartbreaker, since he fears commitment and typically escapes when things seem to be getting too serious.

He has trouble discerning truth from falsehood, which makes him a rather congenial liar. Making a commitment is in direct conflict with his need for freedom and having fun. Unless he overcomes his passive-aggressive behavior, he ultimately fails himself.

Queen of Cups

QUEEN of CUPS.

The Queen of Cups combines imagination with action. She displays unwavering devotion in matters of the heart and provides great emotional support to those whom she loves. She is a loving mother and devoted to her children. She will often be drawn to care professions. In all, she is sensitive, gracious, generous, and kind. She is the first to fight for the underdog.

When she is not at her best, however, she can be a drama queen, powerful but untrustworthy, self-indulgent, impractical, and unfocused. Depression plagues her. She may play the role of an emotional manipulator, who enjoys getting caught up in other people's dramas. When her sexuality is out of control, she may become a seductress or dominatrix, abusing drugs and alcohol.

King of Cups

KING of CUPS.

Responsibility comes before self-expression and personal dreams for the King of Cups, but, in truth, he would rather abdicate. He is a loving and nurturing father and skilled in helping others. However, he finds it difficult to ask for personal support. He is kind, considerate, understanding, and easy to talk to. He tends to veil his emotional intensity, but he is deeply sincere, profoundly caring, and emotionally stable. He may have a secret desire to do something eccentric and outrageous.

When he turns his back on his characteristic good nature, his built-up emotions can become explosive. His repressed feelings and passive-aggressive behavior can manifest as dishonesty, untrustworthiness, and irresponsibility. In a relationship, he may cheat on his partner. He may even turn to alcohol and drug abuse when demands on him become too great.

Ace of Pentacles

ACE of PENTACLES.

THE ROOTS OF THE POWERS OF EARTH

The Ace of Pentacles is bursting with unrealized potential. It is a doorway that may include an inheritance, a successful business opportunity, and promises of prosperity. This Ace is imbued with the hallmarks of safety, security, and comfort. It is infused with the gifts of nature and honors the home as sanctuary. Relationships under the Ace of Pentacles are stable and solid, and pleasures of the body are celebrated. When matters of pregnancy and birth are concerned, a girl may be on the way.

If this Ace is misguided, then what lies in its path may be wealth that corrupts and throwing good money after bad. There is overdependence on material security along with an inordinate fear of leaving the comforts of home.

Two of Pentacles

JUPITER IN CAPRICORN

There is a precarious balance in the Two of Pentacles, though generally a happy one. If you are influenced by the Two of Pentacles, you may be one who makes multitasking look easy. You've learned to go with the flow and be in the moment, welcoming change and trusting the process. Stability and routine bore you. You enjoy taking risks and are willing to roll with the punches. The trick in juggling, however, is knowing which balls are made of rubber and which are made of glass.

You may find yourself in the position of "borrowing from Peter to pay Paul"; you've finally put too many irons in the fire, and you're suffering the consequences. Now you may be pretending to take things lightly, but the game is forced; your enjoyment is feigned once you've realized that while you were playing, you missed an important opportunity.

Three of Pentacles

MARS IN CAPRICORN

The Three of Pentacles proclaims the integration of mind, body, and spirit in the workplace. You have achieved mastery here through hard work, dedication, and working as a team. You take pride in your work and have received well-deserved recognition in your chosen field. Your work is dedicated to the greater good and serving the community.

Unfortunately, when the environment in the workplace is tainted, there may be trouble with coworkers—your efforts produce few results, or you feel that your work goes unappreciated. You may even find yourself out of work altogether.

Four of Pentacles

SUN IN CAPRICORN

In one way, the Four of Pentacles is holding on to money for dear life. If you find yourself under the influence of this card, material comforts equal stability and security, but you may find no joy in your possessions if you're holding on too tightly. What you are unable to give possesses you. Money does not work well as coffin liners.

However, you may also have developed a very respectful approach in regard to your finances, and you are simply making wise choices in order to protect yourself from economic problems down the road. Once you feel sufficiently secure, you may loosen the grip on your purse and realize that there's more to life than money.

Five of Pentacles

MERCURY IN TAURUS

Life is extremely challenging when the Five of Pentacles appears. You may be in a codependent relationship in which the blind is leading the blind. You may be suffering from poverty, illness, or isolation and abandonment, brought on by social stigma. You may be experiencing spiritual starvation.

There is such a long-standing hardship here that you are oblivious to the possible opportunities that are available to you, except perhaps traditional doctrines, which you reject. You may prefer suffering rather than asking for help. Yet, despite your many problems and barely surviving, you are moving forward. You may collapse under overwhelming odds or finally accept help when it is offered to you.

Six of Pentacles

MOON IN TAURUS

Generosity and charity are the hallmarks of the Six of Pentacles. As a benefactor, you are in the privileged position of sharing your wealth. However, as a giver, you have to learn how to set limits, because takers never do. Furthermore, your giving should never foster indolence or dependence or come from a place of ostentation.

If you are on the receiving end of this generosity, caution is advised when you are promised something for nothing. You may become a financial hostage, allowing yourself to be controlled by the unethical tactics of a manipulating charlatan.

Seven of Pentacles

SATURN IN TAURUS

The Seven of Pentacles takes pride in work accomplished. There is healthy growth in an enterprise or relationship. Now it is time for you to take stock before going on to the next step. As you build on your achievements, you may find that you are doing even better than you thought. Slow but steady increase is the name of the game here. Remember, patience is a virtue.

If you become dissatisfied with the slow progress, you may lose sight of your goals, become discouraged, and abandon the project altogether. Time and effort will pay off. Second-guessing your efforts can lead to dissatisfaction and undermine your self-esteem.

Eight of Pentacles

SUN IN VIRGO

Fine craftsmanship as opposed to art is the cornerstone of the Eight of Pentacles. This card may be telling you that it would be a good time to learn a new trade that requires methodical attention to detail. Satisfaction and pride come from a job well done. This is work that serves the community, and grateful recognition is its reward. At the same time, it is important to avoid being married to your work and ignoring your homelife.

If your work turns out to be boring and feels like drudgery, then you may be stuck in a dead-end job that is unsatisfying because it requires no skills. Therefore, you may feel underutilized and insulted by the misuse and abuse of your talents.

Nine of Pentacles

VENUS IN VIRGO

The Nine of Pentacles confirms that you have achieved "the good life," through self-reliance and discipline that is freeing. You are truly at home in the world, blessed with material abundance and a culture-rich environment. You have the air of graceful silence and wordless certainty.

However, loneliness may be a part of achieving your goals. So, you may be rich but alone and longing for companionship to share your abundance. In addition to that, lack of necessity breeds boredom. This may bring into question whether success and sacrifice to achieve it was worth it after all. Perhaps a Welcome sign at the gate would be a place to start.

Ten of Pentacles

MERCURY IN VIRGO

At first glance, the Ten of Pentacles gives the appearance of the established home, which is secure and comfortable. This is the kind of stability that comes from family wealth and tradition. Investments prosper, property is acquired, and there is harmony among generations.

However, if this is all facade, then your loyalty may be more about family duty and waiting for the inheritance, rather than genuine devotion. You may feel trapped by the dependence on old money and find older relatives overbearing and demanding. You may even turn away from the family, chance being disinherited, and pursue a more spiritual path in life.

Page of Pentacles

PAGE of PENTACLES.

The Page of Pentacles is the persevering student, who respects learning and is fascinated by the work itself. He is practical, sensible, diligent, and always ready to please and quick to learn, almost to the point of being overly thorough. He takes life very seriously. He was born with an old head on his young shoulders. He goes cheerfully and dependably about his duties, though at times he may seem a bit shy. He is happiest among family and friends and loves nature and all the comforts that come from physical pleasure.

If he is thrown off track, then he could become scatter-brained, easily distracted, and prone to going off on tangents. His love of life and learning remain endearing, minus the work ethic required to follow through. Or, he may become so obsessed with practicalities that he takes no time off to dream.

Knight of Pentacles

KNIGHT of PENTACLES.

The Knight of Pentacles is hardworking, responsible, humane, uncomplaining, patient, trustworthy, and rooted to the outer world and simplicity. He is dedicated to purely practical matters. He is the enemy of impulse. He is the workhorse who is predictable, unimaginative, and conservative. He follows the rules and is committed to doing the "right" thing. He is a faithful lover, but not terribly exciting.

The Knight of Pentacles can run the gamut from being addicted to work to avoiding responsibility altogether. He can lack class, become a plodder, and deal unethically when it comes to financial matters. Socially, he can be dead weight at gatherings and a couch potato at home. Ideally, he could overturn materialistic obsessions and focus on his inner worth and value.

Queen of Pentacles

QUEEN of PENTACLES.

The Queen of Pentacles is deeply connected to nature and the earth. She is the epitome of the physical expression of love. She is good-hearted, nurturing, self-aware, and sexually fertile. She is a hard worker, with no particular need for recognition or attention. The reward is the work itself. In that regard, she is best described as quietly effective. She is practical and perseveres through chores for the good of herself and others. She is most at home when she is gardening, doing volunteer work, or is in the role of caretaker.

The Queen of Pentacles can become ill at ease when she is cut off from earth connections. She may become stressed or moody, lose her self-confidence, and begin to neglect her responsibilities, particularly if her own physical health is threatened. Domestically, she can ignore her comfortable home, become a stifling mother, or, uncharacteristically, turn into a conspicuous consumer to stave off melancholy.

King of Pentacles

KING of PENTACLES.

The King of Pentacles is a successful business or professional man. He wants the best that can be afforded comfortably. He has the Midas touch with money; he'll take risks, though few and carefully measured. He is a good provider for his family. He has a rather stiff outer shell that hides a heart of gold. He is old-fashioned in his ways and can seem dull and flat. He has no time for frivolity.

The King of Pentacles can develop an overattachment to his possessions and become almost paranoid about losing his wealth or status. At home, he can be a cold and unfeeling father. When he lacks influence or authority and cut off from his wealth, it can manifest in terms of poor health and depression. It may be followed by bad investments, accepting bribes, or becoming miserly.

THE MAJORS

Traditional meanings by author along with the esoteric functions of the Golden Dawn

The Fool

THE FOOL.

NONE

The Fool is a free spirit. He is enthusiastic, fearless, and trusting. He takes chances. He is aptly described as "footloose and fancy free." He lives in the moment, seeking new experiences and adventures. He has a childlike innocence with an uninhibited lust for life. "But what's so beautiful about a fool . . . is that a fool never knows when to give up" (from *Cloud Cuckoo Land* by Anthony Doerr).

However, at times he can be reckless and truly foolish (i.e., "the terminal adolescence"). Or, on the other hand, he may become overly cautious, paranoid, and fearful. Yes, look before you leap, but don't go blind in the process.

The Magician

THE MAGICIAN.

LIFE AND DEATH

The Magician is charming and eloquent. He is well grounded in reality. He gets what he wants, because he knows what he wants. He is effective and inspiring and knows how to make things happen. He is a dynamic communicator, focused and self-confident. His strong willpower makes him a very persuasive communicator. You might see him in the role of performer, writer, artist, teacher, problem solver, or, literally, a magician.

When his positive energy is blocked, he becomes unfocused, apathetic, and depressed and feels weak. Conversely, he may abuse his power or become a con artist, a liar, a trickster, or a swindler.

The High Priestess

PEACE AND WAR

THE HIGH PRIESTESS.

The High Priestess appears enigmatic and unapproachable. She is psychic, intuitive, and mysterious. She keeps her beliefs quietly to herself, living by her actions rather than her words. She is a keeper of secrets and is, therefore, a good listener. She is still, contemplative, meditative, and spiritual.

At times, she can become too reclusive; loneliness and moodiness can set in. At other times, she can become more extroverted and involved. She may appear more passionate and have a deeper involvement with life and other people. While often thought of as the virgin in the Tarot, she may evolve into a more sexually expressive being.

The Empress

WISDOM AND FOLLY

THE EMPRESS.

The Empress is motherhood, Mother Nature, fertility, and the life force. She loves the outdoors and gardening. She is nurturing and protective with unbridled creativity. She can stand for pregnancy or the desire for a child. She can also give birth to an idea. She has a sunny and warm personality and is devoted to her friends and lovers.

At times, she can suppress her emotions and decide she needs some alone time. She can be an overwhelming and smothering mother and wife or behave in a sexually irresponsible way. She may lack charm or become a social climber and neglect her family altogether. This card may also represent feeling unloved by your mother or a broken engagement.

The Emperor

SIGHT

THE EMPEROR.

The Emperor stands for law and order, the rules of society, good judgment, and leadership. He is stable, grounded, and logical and prizes structure. He is willful, wise, and reasonable. This card may come up when issues of father or fatherhood come into play. He is known for his insight, so you may go to him for advice. He always has a rational approach to issues and is analytical rather than emotional. He does everything "by the book." He is "the boss."

He can also become overbearing and rigid, dominating and possessive, a dictator of sorts. He can overintellectualize and become fanatical about "rules." He can hurt others to achieve success, with cruelty disguised as strength. He may also mellow and defer to others. As he grows older he can become senile.

THE HIEROPHANT.

The Hierophant

HEARING

The Hierophant stands for traditional education, teacher/ student relationships, rituals, doctrines, and blind faith. Personal responsibility is surrendered. Conformity rules. The contradictions of life are answered but not solved. He may be a member of the clergy or a guru. The card represents the establishment and marriage.

At other times, he may be a false prophet or an unethical teacher. He may represent unorthodox views or one who questions authority or his faith. He may become more of a free thinker or be more concerned with outer form rather than true spirituality. He may find it difficult to separate from formerly held beliefs that no longer make sense but are part of a tradition.

THE LOVERS.

The Lovers

SMELL

The Lovers follow their hearts. They may be soulmates, married, or in a long-term relationship. Here there is trust, intimacy, and sexuality, with nothing hidden and nothing withheld. There is also cooperation, joining forces, and making important choices. Overall, there is harmony and balance that comes from giving and receiving. Here you may also find the integration of the inner and outer self.

If this relationship breaks down, then there is a kind of destructive love characterized by rejection, lack of cooperation, imbalance, infidelity, or irreconcilable differences. There may be issues with intimacy or sexual incompatibility. You may be allowing a love interest to be a priority when you are only an option.

The Chariot

SPEECH

The Chariot controls feelings and directs the will with self-discipline and decisiveness. Conflicts are controlled but not necessarily resolved. There is a risk here of being too rigid. However, the Chariot moves forward despite conflicts. There is a unification of opposites directed by unstoppable drive and single-mindedness.

When the Chariot is derailed, conflicts may become overwhelming. Courage is replaced by weakness and feeling out of control. There may also be a sudden outburst of anger or forcefully imposing your will. Under those circumstances, power is replaced by arrogance, selfishness, and overaspiration. On a more literal level, there may be travel to a known destination, car trouble, or a delayed or canceled trip.

Strength

TASTE

Strength is about imposing your higher will of your lower nature. Strength is imbued with love and gentle understanding that comes from strength from within. Strength knows how to transform enemies into peaceful allies with loving firmness. She is quietly effective and self-disciplined. She faces life passionately but peacefully. She is a lovely lady with the heart of a lion.

This card can also be about overcoming addiction of various kinds. Strength can feign weakness to manipulate others, or become openly aggressive and abuse her power. Under those circumstances, her lower instincts trump her higher will. Strength may show her vulnerable side by seeking help and support when the courage to face life fails, leaving her feeling weak, overwhelmed, and pessimistic.

The Hermit

SEXUALITY (TOUCH)

The Hermit is searching for self-knowledge, wisdom, and enlightenment. He is a seeker, a guide, a guru, and a giver of light. This may be a time for you to withdraw from the outer world to seek inner truth by journeying to a spiritual retreat. It is a time for solitude and isolation, a "time-out" for contemplation.

The Hermit may also be a roamer, running away from problems and refusing the call. He can become too isolated from others and literally become a hermit. He may be a false prophet or question his spirituality. The Hermit can fear old age and being alone or have a paranoid fear of other people. This also can be a time when he reaches out and becomes more involved in society.

The Wheel of Fortune

RICHES AND POVERTY

The Wheel of Fortune points to a turning point for better or worse. It is time to roll with the punches and remember that this too shall pass. "Pride cometh before a fall." The Wheel suggests a second chance, or what goes around comes around. Be prepared for new cycles with life's ups and downs and learn from the experience.

The Wheel of Fortune may also bring unexpected good luck. Attempting to resist change will send the wheel spinning out of control and literally going around in circles. Expect the inevitability of change and setbacks. Pick yourself up, brush yourself off, and start all over again.

Justice

JUSTICE.

WORK

Justice brings with her balance and fair play. Absolute honesty, levelheadedness, and a just decision are absolute. Justice is a seeker of truth and pursues it with impartial scrutiny. This may also indicate an encounter with law enforcement or courts, negotiating a compromise, or arbitration.

If Justice is not true to her nature, then there may be unfair judgments or punishments. There may be indications of unethical behavior, corruption in the law, or leaping to a hasty decision. Justice may be a pretense, with the outcome already decided, or forcing one's version of the truth onto others.

The Hanged Man

THE HANGED MAN.

NONE

The Hanged Man represents a spiritual awakening that entails withdrawing from society to search for your inner truth. There is a commitment to your own convictions regardless of how they are viewed by the world. The Hanged Man is an independent thinker who lives to the beat of a different drummer. It is a time of inner transformation, letting go of control and thus achieving it. Surrender to the Higher Power. There is progress in apparent stillness, attainment in sacrifice. This may be a time to turn a problem on its head in order to look at it differently and, perhaps, more clearly.

When the Hanged Man succumbs to social pressures, he denies his inner truth and questions whether the sacrifice is worth it. He may become fanatical about spiritual pursuits or become "hung up" between two ways of thinking. There is also a danger of remaining still for too long; it is time to reap what you have sown.

Death

DEATH.

MOVEMENT

The Death card marks endings, change, movement, new beginnings, afterlife, and death. It may also indicate that it is time to let go of the past and close those doors so that others can be opened. Death may serve as a doorway to liberation from what has been fixed. Now may be a time to release restricting habits and obsolete ways.

Death may also suggest a fear of death or denying your mortality. It may point to stagnation, a sluggish and boring life, or resistance to change.

Temperance

TEMPERANCE.

ANGER

Temperance points to the blending of opposites, balance in the face of extremes, self-control, and anger management. Temperance can be a negotiator or a diplomat. Spontaneity is combined with knowledge. There are also associations with health, healing, and flexible strength.

The downside of Temperance can manifest as anger, lack of self-restraint, and going to extremes in a life that is out of balance and out of control. In terms of your well-being, it can indicate poor health, blocked energy, stress, or addiction. Blocked emotions can lead to depression or violence.

The Devil

LAUGHTER

The Devil is all about temptation, obsession, libido, self-limiting behavior, and indulgences. The Devil displays an attractive surface appearance through his sense of fun and laughter. He is a charmer, that's for sure. But if one looks deeper, there's a sense of feeling chained, imprisoned, trapped, and spiritually empty. You can become a slave to your desires with drugs, bondage, and S&M sex to the extent that desires overpower judgment.

If the Devil is rehabilitated, there's the possibility of fighting off the demons, confronting the dark side, and unleashing the Devil's hold. You may pursue a healthier lifestyle, which includes finding spirituality and loving yourself and others. For those with various forms of addiction, therapy may be indicated.

THE TOWER.

The Tower

INDIGNATION AND GRACE

With the Tower comes violent upheaval, literal or psychological, which may take the form of a tumultuous breakup of a relationship or any other sort of revelation that hits like a lightning bolt. This is an Aha! moment in life. It is helpful to keep in mind that to live the ultimate dream is to face the ultimate nightmare. The result is an epiphany, which is meant to enlighten, not destroy.

However, if you stay so tightly controlled, there is no room for growth. Seize the day or it will seize you. The Tower can be a blessing in disguise. By overcoming ego and facing beliefs that are based on false assumptions, you can connect to the higher power of enlightenment.

THE STAR.

The Star

IMAGINATION

The Star brings openness, freedom, an inner calm, and the loss of pretense. This is a time for seeing yourself as part of nature and the accompanying humility. It promises hope, especially after an upheaval. As a humanitarian, it gives and expects nothing in return. The Star may recommend seeking calm surroundings for meditation and contemplating new beginnings. The Star also provides an opportunity to "shine," particularly in the area of the arts. "Hope sees the invisible; feels the intangible; achieves the impossible." —Anonymous.

If the Star is not shining brightly, then this could be a time of shame, depression, feeling closed off, and the accompanying low self-esteem. You may lose hope by denying your true gift when you are cut off from your source of inspiration.

THE MOON.

The Moon

SLEEP

When the Moon appears, it may bring with it strange emotions, dreams, fears, visions, and hallucinations. You may find that you are struggling with the wild and the tame within yourself. The Moon may also have a calming effect, which can awaken the unconscious and open up channels of psychic energy and pure intuition. The Moon also speaks of cycles (i.e., female cycles).

When the Moon is to your detriment, you may have difficulty sleeping, experience nightmares, feel psychically drained, or be prone to compulsive lying. Under its extreme influence, insanity may prevail. There may be indulgences in secret addictions to escape the demons and avoid "the things that go bump in the night."

THE SUN.

The Sun

FERTILITY AND BARRENNESS

The Sun is very optimistic and brings with it an array of positive energy: joy, freedom from limitations, boundless energy, self-confidence, enthusiasm, good health, and childlike excitement. You will undoubtedly be drawn to the Sun, because of the life-affirming radiance it exudes. Even on a cloudy day, the sun continues to shine, but perhaps not quite so brightly.

Happiness may be slightly diminished. There may be some loss of interest in life. Joy requires more effort to achieve. The childish side of the Sun may appear and show its immaturity and inflated ego or discover that it is too innocent to live in a dangerous world. Issues concerning your health may surface. Since the Sun exposes all there is to see, the dark side may now be exposed. That said, the Sun is still a very positive card.

Judgement

JUDGEMENT.

NONE

Judgement is a wake-up call, a time for starting over. It is a radical change from the past. It says that now is the time to shed old ways of believing and thinking and rise to your higher nature. This is a true calling, but you must heed the call. As a result of this revelation, decisions and choices must be made if you are to journey to higher spiritual ground.

If you choose to ignore the call for fear of the unknown or are resistant to change, your life remains at a standstill with all the accompanying limitations. It may be a case of "The spirit is willing, but the flesh is weak." There are growing pains to be sure, but remember, "No pain, no gain."

The World

THE WORLD.

POWER AND SERVITUDE

"All's right with the World!" comes to mind when this card appears. Here, you will experience a wonderful sense of well-being, exhilaration, and fulfillment. You have truly found your bliss and are at one with the world. Life is good! This full circle brings with it joyous victories, total self-acceptance, and commitment to a future of limitless possibilities.

Should you succumb to the negative energy of this card, the world may have turned upside down. Life can be riddled with self-doubt and impatience when progress is slow. Your willpower and drive may have been replaced with perceived limitations and stagnation. However, the World will rebound. The dance of life may be delayed, but it will resume.

INTRODUCTION TO ILLUSTRATIONS

It would be remiss of me if I did not include the wonderful Pamela Colman Smith illustrations I referenced in the introduction. They are particularly relevant to this writing because they are not drawn from her work as a Tarot illustrator.

Smith was influenced in her artistic style by "the Arts and Crafts movement," which was very popular between 1880 and 1910. At the core of this method was the use of delineated, simplified forms, defining flat areas of color.

Her education in this system was developed during the time that she was studying art at the Pratt Institute in Brooklyn, New York, from 1893 to 1897.

Robert M. Place, noted art scholar, author, and deck designer, remarked that some of these paintings show the influence of Japanese prints. It is known that Arthur Wesley Dow, her teacher at the Pratt Institute, was heavily influenced by these prints and would have introduced her to them. Place goes on to say that Smith was also swayed by the art nouveau style; that inspiration is evidenced in the painting of Ellen Terry (see appendix III, Fourth image). This elegant and playful interpretation has such an "Off with you" and "Devil may care" kind of whimsical sense of humor. The colors are bright and joyful and gleefully glide about the canvas. (Read a more in-depth commentary, "Pamela Colman Smith and the Arts and Crafts Movement," by Robert M. Place, which follows this introduction.)

The renderings of her other characters, some of which are almost folktale in style, breathe three-dimensional life. Notice the brightly colored painting of the eloping (my interpretation) couple, the joyful satisfaction on their faces as they escape the grips of her winded father, helplessly chasing after them in clouds of dust, as they merrily gallop away. In one moment, captured as if a still in a storybook, Smith tells a wonderfully delightful story in a single glace: Plot, Character, Theme, Atmosphere, with Costume and Scenery (see appendix III, Third image).

In stark contrast (see appendix III, Second image), there is the bleak-looking hill top with a mournful figure casting her eyes away from the ships below that are sailing out to sea. The tone and style here are dramatically different from the one described above. One would have no trouble imagining this figure's state of being. The color palette is awash with muted maroons and shades of gray.

Did this painting inspire Smith's Two of Wands? It is certainly reminiscent.

Actually, a number of these illustrations led my imaginings to other Tarot cards: the all-black-and-gray illustration of a woman slightly bowing before a lifeless tree, with three female characters clinging closely behind her. Could it be the Three of Cups reversed? The three women in the background mourning the ghost of one of them who has departed? Or the Four of Cups? My mind also wanders to the scene that we might have observed soon after the Crucifixion (see appendix III, First image).

Most of these illustrations show Smith unbridled, free of the constraints that designing the Tarot cards may have placed on her. Of course, there are always some guidelines when illustrating a book, or creating a painting that was commissioned by a client.

Nonetheless, we see here how wonderfully diverse this set of illustrations is. Her heretofore unheralded artistry has finally taken center stage. She has earned this standing ovation!

"PAMELA COLMAN SMITH AND THE ARTS AND CRAFTS MOVEMENT"

By Robert M. Place
Creator of *The Alchemical Tarot*
author of *The Tarot, History, Symbolism and Divination*

In 1891, Arthur Edward Waite, the occult author known for his translations of the works of Levi, Papus, and numerous alchemical texts, joined the English occult society named the Hermetic Order of Golden Dawn. At first, The Golden Dawn had three branches, called temples. The London branch that Waite belonged to was called the Isis-Urania Temple. This temple also included several prominent artists such as the Irish poet W. B. Yates as members. In 1903, the temple split into two splinter groups. The group that retained the name, Isis-Urania, was headed by Yates, and its focus was on ritual magic. Waite headed the second group, called the Independent and Rectified Order of The Golden Dawn.

Although Waite was an occultist, he mainly focused on the occult practice of white magic or mysticism. He believed that the true goal of occult ritual was spiritual transformation and enlightenment, not manipulative magic, which he categorized as debased. Under Waite's leadership, his faction became devoted to ceremonial practices that could be viewed as a new mystical religion—an occult version of Catholicism.

In 1901, Pamela Colman Smith, who had established herself as a talented artist, illustrator, miniature theater designer, and storyteller, joined the Isis-Urania Temple. It is likely that this decision was influenced by her friendship with William Butler Yates and his brother Jack. However, in 1903, she chose to be in Waite's group instead of Yates's group. After this, her friendship with Yates waned. Waite took notice of the talented artist in his group. Later, in his memoirs, he expressed both his confidence in her artistic abilities, but also some unfounded doubts about her intellectual ability.

"Now in those days there was a most imaginative and abnormally psychic artist named Pamela Colman Smith, who had drifted into The Golden Dawn and loved the ceremonies—as transformed by myself—without pretending or indeed attempting to understand their sub-surface consequence. It seemed to some of us in the circle that there was a draftswoman among us who, under proper guidance, could produce a Tarot with an appeal to the world of art and a suggestion of the significance behind the Symbols which would put on them another construction than had ever been dreamed by those who, through many generations, had produced and used them for mere divinatory purposes." (Waite, Arthur Edward; *Shadows of Life and Thought*; Kessinger Publishing; p. 184)

We can also see in this quote that Waite included divination in his list of debased magical practices. His interest in the Tarot was based on his belief that it illustrated the mystical quest for enlightenment, and he believed that Smith was the artist who had the talent to illuminate that aspect.

Although I don't share Waite's professed distaste for divination, I agree with him that the Tarot illustrates the mystical quest. This is the basis for my creation of *The Alchemical Tarot*, which correlates the Tarot trumps with the alchemical Great Work. Also, I feel that Waite's distaste for divination was contrived. He actually wrote a book on cartomancy under the pen name Grand Orient and had the audacity to quote Grand Orient as an expert in his *Pictorial Key to the Tarot*. As Scott Martin points out in this book, the inclusion of theatrical fully illustrated pips made The Waite Smith Tarot one of the best decks for divination and accounts for its world-wide reputation. Waite certainly endorsed this aspect of the deck that he commissioned.

I appreciate Waite, and I often quote him in my books, but again I have to take exception to his underappreciation of Smith's insight into the deeper meaning of the Tarot's symbols. I believe that Smith was actually heir to a mystical artistic tradition that can be traced back to alchemy and that created the cultural conditions in England that allowed The Golden Dawn to exist. This mystical tradition was more deeply ingrained in Smith, and her artwork was a purer expression of that tradition than were Waite's prose. To explain this view, I need to digress. So, bear with me while I discuss alchemy and artistic traditions in the seventeenth century.

Paracelsus was the most famous Renaissance alchemist. Born in Basel, in 1493, he received a doctorate at age sixteen from the University of Ferrara and wandered Europe practicing medicine, botany, astrology, magic, and alchemy. He grounded alchemy in Hermetic philosophy, and instead of trying to make gold or searching for the traditional one magical panacea, he sought practical cures for illness. He is considered the founder of modern medicine. After Paracelsus, alchemy split in two directions: those who continued to work in the lab attempting to make gold and those who abandoned the lab for the philosophical pursuit of spiritual gold.

Physical alchemy, as practiced in the lab, did not do well in the seventeenth century. There were numerous "puffers," called this because they only saw alchemy as a way to get rich quick by creating gold, but beside the puffers, there were others who were actual con men, who used false claims of transmutation to dupe gullible investors. In England, the Royal Society cast doubts on the possibility of creating gold, and in 1661, Robert Boyle wrote *The Skeptical Chemist*, in which he demonstrated that the classical four elements could be broken down into smaller elements. Scientists redefined an element as these smaller irreducible particles and created the periodic table. In this period, called the "Age of Enlightenment," scientific reason and logic progressed and there was a turning away from alchemy, magic, and mysticism in Western culture.

On the other hand, the philosophical approach to alchemy did manage to bear fruit and feed the need for inner truth beyond the materialistic rationalism of science. One aspect was the creation of mystical societies such as the Rosicrucian Brotherhood in Germany and the Freemasons in England. Many later occult societies claimed to derive from the original Rosicrucians. The largest and most influential was the Hermetic Order of The Golden Dawn.

Philosophical alchemy, however, was primarily exemplified by two German mystics: Michael Maier (1565–1622) and Jacob Bohme (1575–1624). Maier was a physician, who worked for Emperor Rudolf II in Prague. Bohme was a Lutheran shoemaker and a natural mystic, who had a life-changing vision while contemplating sunlight reflected in a pewter dish. Both men authored numerous alchemical texts, which are noted for their enigmatic engraved illustrations. Maier, in particular, is the author of Atalanta Fugiens, 1618. With its richly engraved illustrations of dreamlike surreal imagery and a text composed of poems, prose, and music scores, Atalanta Fugiens is a multidimensional work of art. Both of these alchemists had a tremendous influence on German poets and artists and helped to create the Romantic Movement in art. As alchemy faded, it was replaced by art.

Romanticism rejected the rational approach of the Enlightenment and was naturally allied with alchemical or Hermetic themes and symbols. It was an artistic, literary, musical, and intellectual movement that flourished in Western Europe and was at its peak from 1790 to 1840, with artists such as Caspar David Friedrich, Henry Fuseli, and William Blake. But it can be seen as an ongoing influence on the arts into the twentieth century and is still with us today. In the broadest sense it may include The Hudson River School in the United States, founded by Thomas Cole, the Pre-Raphaelites in England, exemplified by Dante Gabriel Rossetti, and the Symbolists artists in late[-]nineteenth[-]century Europe, such as Gustave Moreau or Arnold Böcklin.

Romanticism was characterized by its emphasis on individualism and emotions such as fear, horror, awe, and the esthetic experience. It glorified the sublime beauty of nature, and the past, preferring the Medieval period over the Classical, which was associated with the scientific rationalization of nature. It reacted against the mechanization and monotony of the Industrial Revolution. It also embraced Hermetic philosophy, particularly the belief that nature was a living presence filled with living matter, that there was a connection between human emotions and the physical world, and that imagination was to be valued.

Now let us focus on nineteenth[-]century England and the Pre-Raphaelites Brotherhood, founded in 1848. Like the Rosicrucians, the Pre-Raphaelites were a mystical brotherhood, but composed of painters, poets, and art critics, and eventually came to include woman as well as men. The Pre-Raphaelites sought a return to the sincerity of the detailed compositions and pure colors of fifteenth-century Italian art, the same period that gave us the Tarot. They rejected what they regarded as the mechanistic approach first adopted by Mannerist artists who succeeded Raphael. They believed the classical stylistic compositions of Raphael had been a corrupting influence on art. They also believed that art was a spiritual or magical endeavor, a doorway to the inner realm of the psyche. Their works often illustrated myths and legends, such as the quest of the Grail, and they created a romantic but realistically rendered image of the Middle Ages. The most famous Pre-Raphaelite artists of the first generation were: William Holman Hunt (1827–1910), John Everett Millais (1829–1896), and Dante Gabriel Rossetti (1828–1882). The second generation included: Rossetti's disciples Edward Burne-Jones (1833–1898) and William Morris (1834–1896). It was the work of these artists and mystics that helped to create the fertile soil in England in which The Golden Dawn took root.

One of the most enduring products of Pre-Raphaelite art was the creation of the Arts and Crafts Movement. The prominent art critic, John Ruskin, was an avid supporter of the Pre-Raphaelites. He despised what the Industrial Revolution was doing to the quality of life and the moral health of the nation and wanted society to return to the purity and beauty of the romantic Medieval vision that he found in the works of the Pre-Raphaelites and in Gothic Revival architecture. Ruskin considered industrial mechanized production and division of labor to be dehumanizing. He believed that the health of the society and of the individual required workers to design the things that they made, and to create their designs with handwork and craft. In this way, common functional objects would become individually designed and skillfully created works of art that would enhance the lives of their recipients as well as their creators.

William Morris was a devotee of Ruskin's views and founded a company for the creation of handcrafted furniture, stained glass, and tapestries. He enlisted his friend Burne-Jones as a partner and a designer, particularly for the imagery on his tapestries and windows. In 1891, he created the publishing company, Kelmscott Press, dedicated to creating beautiful, handcrafted books printed in letter press on handmade paper or vellum with woodcut illustrations and decorative borders. He printed over fifty titles, which included Medieval texts, the works of Romantic poets, and his own work. Again, he enlisted Burne-Jones to create the illustrations, as well as the younger artist Walter Crane, who had briefly apprenticed with Burne-Jones. Crane was a famous illustrator, particularly noted for his children's books, and he also embraced the Arts and Crafts movement. In 1887, Crane had presided as the president over the founding of the Arts and Crafts Exhibition Society, which held exhibitions in London until 1916. It was this Society that gave the name Arts and Crafts to the movement. Along with their work as artists, both Morris and Crane were active in the Socialist League, a political movement advocating a socialist proletarian revolution that would protect the rights of workers and the nobility of labor, views that were in harmony with Arts and Crafts.

The Arts and Crafts movement spread through England and into Scotland[,] where it is exemplified in the Glasgow School and the work of Charles Rennie Mackintosh, whose work displays the Japanese influences that were prevalent in the late nineteenth century and that bridges into the Art Nouveau movement in decorative arts. Morris's writing on crafts also helped initiate the crafts revival in India and Japan. In the United States it was promoted by Gustave Stickley, of New York, who developed the Crafts-man Style of furniture and architecture, and published The Craftsman magazine from 1901 to 1916. One branch of Craftsman architecture was the Prairie School, which included Frank Lloyd Wright's early work. Later in the twentieth century, the Craftsman style and the concern for handcrafts gave birth to the American Craft Movement that I was part of for twenty years.

Now that we have established what the Arts and Crafts Movement is and what it is heir to, it is time to discuss Pamela Colman Smith and her contribution to the movement.

Pamela Colman Smith was born in London in 1878. Her parents, Corinne Colman Smith and Charles Edward Smith, were from prominent Brooklyn Heights families and followers of the mystical teachings of the Swedish philosopher and psychic Eman-uel Swedenborg. Pamela's grandfather was a prominent publisher of Swedenborg lit-erature in the US, her grandmother was a children's book author, and her uncle was a member of the Hudson River School of landscape painters. Among her family ties she could count William Gillette, an actor famous for his portrayal of Sherlock Holmes. Pamela's mother also performed as an actress, and her father was a world traveler with a large collection of Japanese Ukiyo-e woodblock prints.

In 1881, Pamela's family settled in Manchester, England. Her father was a pros-perous manager in the textile industry. The textile workers in Manchester were immersed in the Arts and Crafts Movement, which they saw as the cure for the drudgery of factory work. Possibly because of the high rate of early deaths among the workers, interest in spiritualism was also prevalent. This was Pamela's environment in her for-mative years. When Pamela was ten years old, her father took a job with the West India Improvement Company, and the family moved to Jamaica. Jamaican culture and folklore had a life-long influence on her work, and she would later perform and pub-lish books of stories on Annancy, the spider trickster, and other Jamaican myths.

In 1893, when she was fifteen, she moved to New York and enrolled at Pratt Insti-tute, in Brooklyn, where she studied art until 1987. During this period, she traveled back and forth between Jamaica and Brooklyn and continued her studies. She returned to Jamaica briefly in 1896 to nurse her sick mother, but her mother died in July.

At that time, many students at Pratt were influenced by the Pre-Raphaelites and working in that style. Pamela was no exception. She started creating works with Me-dieval themes, including portraits of Merlin, Vivian, Guinevere, and images of fairies. It was at school that she also created her first miniature theater. The curriculum at Pratt was strongly influenced by the ideals of the Arts and Crafts Movement. It stressed the integration of fine art and industrial design, and the belief that art could enhance the lives of all classes of people. They believed that art and beauty is the cure for an imbal-anced overly materialistic society, that the esthetic experience was a healing experience, and they valued individual imagination and creativity.

Perhaps Pamela's biggest influence came when she studied with Arthur Wesley Dow. Dow was a leading figure in the American Arts and Crafts Movement. He advocated purity of design based on formal elements, such as line, color, and form that were to be worked into a dynamic composition. He also stressed the importance of handwork and that art needed to be a living force in everyday life. Dow's ideas were ahead of his time and became the bases of Modern Art esthetics in the twentieth century. Much of his esthetic theory was developed while studying his extensive collection of Japanese Ukiyo-e prints. Pamela grew up with Japanese prints and quickly absorbed Dow's lessons. We can see this Japanese influence in her early work in her use of heavy delineating lines, flat areas of color, and compositions that crop through figures to create a well-balanced composition but to also suggest that the scene continues past the frame of the illustration.

As a professional artist, Pamela focused on illustration and theater design. She illustrated numerous literary projects, such as The Illustrated Versus of William Butler Yeats, and a collection of West Indian folktales that she authored called Annancy Stories. The same year that Annancy Stories was published, 1899, thanks to her father's connections, Pamela was introduced to Henry Erving and Ellen Terry, who happened to be the most famous actors in England. She also developed a close relationship with Terry's daughter, Edith Craig. Because of these connections Pamela was invited to create an illustrated brochure for the Lyceum Theater that featured intimate renderings of Erving and Terry during performances. For a brief time, she worked with Jack Yates, W. B. Yates's brother, to publish A Broad Sheet, a one-page bulletin that featured illustrations and poetry. Later she produced her own multi-paged publication called The Green Leaf. Being true to her Arts and Crafts ideals, each publication that she worked on was printed in letter press on a hand press, and every page was hand colored with opaque or transparent watercolors.

In London, Pamela became part of the "in-crowd" of artists, writers, and musicians, associated with the Yates family. In 1901, she was invited to join the Irish Literary Society and the Masquers, which included Walter Crane in its membership. After her Tarot deck was completed, in December, 1909, she was invited to exhibit the deck in Crane's Arts and Crafts Exhibition, demonstrating that the deck was accepted as an example of Arts and Crafts. We can find evidence that her work was exhibited again in the Exhibition in 1914.

One of the most important influences that Dow had on Pamela was that he introduced her to the concept of synesthesia in art. Synesthesia happens when one sense, such as hearing, stimulates another sense, such as vision. For example, sounds may be experienced as colors. Dow encouraged his students to experience music visually. After the demise of The Green Leaf, in 1900, when she was staying at Ellen Terry's home in Smallhythe, near Kent, Pamela began experimenting with this technique while listening to Bach. The result was a vision of frolicking fairies. She soon accumulated a collection of visionary works based on listening to music. These were some of her most successful paintings and, in 1907, they led to her having an exhibition of her work in the gallery of the famous photographer, Alfred Stieglitz, in New York. The gallery was called the Photo-Secession or Gallery 291, and she was the first painter to be exhibited. The show received critical acclaim and her work was reviewed in the March issue of Stickley's The Craftsman, along with two reproductions of her work and a one-page article written by Pamela, encouraging artists to overcome fear.

This brings us to 1909, when Waite hired Pamela for, in her words, "very little money," to create The Waite Smith Tarot. The deck was first published in England in 1909 by William Rider & Sons. This is the copy that was exhibited in the Arts and Crafts Exhibition. It was called The Tarot or the "rectified" Tarot Deck. In 1971, when the deck was republished in the United States by U.S. Games, the title was The Rider Tarot. U.S. Games had previously republished the 1JJ Swiss Tarot and they distinguished Smith's deck by including the name of the original English publisher. This was probably not a good selling point, so they quickly changed the name to The Rider Waite Tarot.

This title gave many people the false impression that it was Waite who designed the cards. Even in new books on the deck[,] we find authors wondering what Waite intended when he included some minor detail on a card, which in reality I doubt that he ever noticed. To design a work of art you need to actually create it or draw a detailed plan that other artists can follow, and Waite is not known to have ever drawn anything. He hired Smith to design the deck because he recognized that she was a gifted artist, and he was not. Some may claim that Smith was working under Waite's close supervision. But Waite and Smith were not even in the same city for the six months that she worked on the deck. She was in Smallhythe, and Waite was in London. She only had a few months to complete the project and the kind of work that she did, in pen and ink and watercolor, cannot be edited without scraping the piece and starting over, so it is doubtful that Waite had much influence.

In his memoirs, Waite admitted that Pamela was intuitive and not someone who could easily be directed. He did try to "spoon feed" her details for three trump cards: the High Priestess, the Fool, and the Hanged Man, but those were the only ones, and the reason that he gave was that Pamela was so psychic that he feared she would uncover more than he told her and expose secrets that he was sworn not to reveal. When describing the cards in The Pictorial Key to the Tarot, Waite often misinterprets the images, not noticing relevant details and even describing details that are not there. This is even true on trump cards, such as the Charioteer, whom he describes as holding a sword that is not there, and the Devil, whom he says has a caduceus rising from his groin, a description of a detail in Levi's "Baphomet," which is one model for the Devil, but not present on Pamela's card.

The first article ever written about the deck was an article by Waite published in the December, 1909 edition of The Occult Review, also published by Rider. In his introduction for the article, Ralph Shirley, the editor of the magazine, mentions that it is accompanied by new Tarot images designed by Pamela Colman Smith, who also researched Renaissance decks for the project. Here are his exact words:

"I have the pleasure to announce to my readers the forthcoming publication of a new pack of Tarot Cards, an illustrated notice of which under the title of the *Tarot; a Wheel of Fortune*, by Mr. A. E. Waite, appears in the current number of this magazine. The Cards will, I anticipate, be ready for sale by about December 10. These can be better judged by the illustrations which go with the article in this issue than by any description I can give them.* It will, however, be apparent that they are of a far higher quality in respect of artistic merit than any pack which has hitherto been published. The Cards in their published form will be fully coloured. The lithographing process has been undertaken by Messers. Sprague & Co., whose name is sufficient guarantee for the excellence of the work. Simultaneously with the issue of these Cards there will be published a book entitled *The Key to the Tarot*, to be sold in a case along with the pack for 7s. post free."

*I may mention that the artist, Miss Colman Smith, made a careful examination of numerous Tarot packs from the fourteenth century onwards before undertaking her work.

(Shirley, Ralph; "Notes of the Month," *The Occult Review*; William Rider & Sons; December, 1909; pages 300–301)

All the ads for the deck in later issues of *The Occult Review* clearly state that they were designed by Pamela Colman Smith. Yet, it is only recently that authors and publishers have added Smith's name to the deck to again honor her as the designer. Not only did Pamela Colman Smith design the deck that now sometimes bears her name, but I feel that I have made the case that she was a visionary working is a tradition that is rooted in alchemy and Western mysticism. And it is the visionary power and simplicity of her designs that has made it the most popular Tarot deck in the world.

—Robert M. Place,
Designer of *The Alchemical Tarot* and author of *The Tarot, History, Symbolism, and Divination*

PAMELA COLMAN SMITH ART EXHIBIT, PRATT ART INSTITUTE—JANUARY 2019

PAMELA COLMAN SMITH

LIFE AND WORK

PRATT INSTITUTE LIBRARIES
Brooklyn Campus Library
200 WILLOUGHBY AVE, BROOKLYN

Opening Reception & Tarot Reading:
Thursday, January 31, 2019, 5:00-8:00 PM

On View:
Thursday, January 31-April 4, 2019
Open During Libary Hours

CURATED BY
COLLEEN LYNCH &
MELISSA STAIGER

According to Pamela Colman Smith, the Untold Story: "Untitled drawing by Pamela Colman Smith. From the collection of Dorothy Norman, 1997. Courtesy of Philadelphia Museum of Art." Our description could read, "Untitled drawing by Pamela Colman Smith."

Second image: Same source. "Beethoven Sonata No. 11. watercolor on paper board by Pamela Colman Smith. Courtesy of The Beineacke Rare Book and Manuscript Library, Yale University."

Our description could read, "Beethoven Sonata No. 11, watercolor by Pamela Colman Smith." or just "Watercolor by Pamela Colman Smith."

Third Image; Same source. An illustration by Pamela Colman Smith from the song "Widdi-combe Fair," 1899 Third image: Same

Fourth image: Pratt Exhibit-Pamela Colman Smith—Life and Work. Ellen Terry, a late-nine-teenth- to early-twentieth-century English actress and friend of Smith.

SHOULD THE ART STUDENT THINK?

By Pamela Colman Smith
The Craftsman 14, no. 4 (July 1908)
Published by Gustav Stickley, 29 W. 34th St., New York

All you students who are just beginning your work in Art School, stop—think! First make sure in your own mind that what end you wish to work for. Do you know? Perhaps you have not decided. You will leave all that to time when you have learned to draw and leave the school—a crippled tool—ready to begin your serious work and have a studio and all the rest of it. Do not wait till then! Put in a corner of your mind an idea such as "I wish to paint portraits." Just keep that idea in the corner, and do not forget that it is there. Call it up sometimes and review your work in front of it. Thus, am I working at the faces of all the people I see—trying to find out their character, imagining how I should paint them if I were to do so? Am I trying to show more of their character than appears on the surface? Can I see it? No. But how shall I find it? Look for it.

When you see a portrait of an historical person, note the dress, the type of face; see if you can trace the character in the face; note the pose, for often pose will date a picture as correctly as the hair or clothes. . . . Remember the date, if the picture is dated; if not, place it in your mind as a second half of the fourteenth century, or the first half of the eighteenth, and so on. If you are not sure of the period, make a pencil sketch and take it with you to some reference library. Once a week make it a point of looking up all the clothes you have seen (or wish to draw in some composition perhaps). Some day when you may have a novel to illustrate and a character to portray, you will remember, "Oh, yes, a dress of the kind worn by so and so in the portrait by so and so— that type—or no! Somewhat more lively."

Go and see all the plays you can. For the stage is a great school or should be to the illustrator, as well as to others. First watch the simple forms of joy, fear, of sorrow; look at the position taken by the whole body, then the face—but that can come afterward.

As an exercise draw a composition of fear or sadness, or great sorrow; quite simply, do not bother about details now, but in a few lines tell your story. Then show it to any one of your friends, or family, or fellow students, and ask them if they can tell you what it is you meant to portray. You will soon get to know how to make it tell its tale. After you have found how to tell a simple story, put in more details, the face, and indicate the dress. Next time you go to the play look at the clothes, hat, cloak, armor, belt, sword, dagger, rings, boots jewels. Watch how the cloak swings when the person walks, how the hands are used. See if you can judge if clothes are correct, or if they are worn correctly; for they are often ruined by the way that they are put on. An actor should be able to show the period and manner of the time in the way he puts on his clothes, as well the way he uses his hands, head, legs.

This may be beside the mark, think you! "Of what use is the stage to me? I am to be an illustrator of books! The stage is false, exaggerated, unreal," you say. So are a great many pictures in books, and the books, too, for that matter. The stage has taught me almost all I know of clothes, of action and of pictorial gestures.

Learn from everything, see everything, and above all feel everything! And make other people when they look at your drawing feel it too!

Make your training at your art school your a b c. You must learn to hold a brush, to mix paint, to draw in perspective, and study anatomy.

Keep an open mind to all things. Hear all you can, good music, for sound and form are more closely connected that we know.

Think good thoughts of beautiful things, colors, sounds, places, no mean thoughts. When you see a lot of dirty people in a crowd, do not remember only the dirt, but the great spirit that is in them all, and the power that they represent.

For through ugliness is beauty sometimes found. Lately I have seen a play, ugly, passionate, realistic, brutal. All through that play I felt that ugly things may be true to nature, but surely it is through evil, that we realize good. The far-off scent of morning air, the blue mountains, the sunshine, the flowers, of a country I once lived in, seemed to rise before me—and there on the stage was a woman sitting on a chair, her body stiff, her eyes rolling, a wonderfully realistic picture of a fit.

I believe that in the so-called composition class, the future of many a student lies. (Professor Arthur Dow, of Columbia University, has proved this, and through his influence I believe a good many schools have begun to teach composition first.)

But let the student begin young, and with all the necessary aids for the broadening of his mind. Composition first, and all the other rules and rudiments, in order as they come. As much literature, music drama as possible (all to be thought of in relation to that idea so safely tucked away in the corner of the student's mind), to be worked at from the vantage point of knowing what they are to aid.

I wish here to say how grateful I am to the writer of an article in an American magazine (*Putman's Monthly* for July 1907). "An appreciation of Albert Sterner, and a protest against the 'ultra-sweetness and oppressive propriety' admired alike by the 'publisher and the public,' and 'individuality discreetly suppressed.'"

O! the prudishness and pompous falseness of a great mass of intelligent people! I do not hold that "the incessant roar of high-power presses" is alone to blame for the stifling of life, but for a lack of inspiration. For it is a land of power, a land of unkempt uproar of life, force, energy.

Lift up your ideals, you weaklings, and force a way out of that thunderous clamor of the steam press, the hurrying herd of blind humanity, noise, dust, strife, seething toil—there is power! The imprisoned Titans underneath the soil, grinding, writhing—take your strength from them, throw aside your petty drawing room point of view.

I do not want to see riotous, clumsy, ugliness suddenly spring up, but a fine noble power shining through your work. The illustrations that I see in the magazines by the younger people are all dignified and well, carefully and conscientiously drawn—but their appalling clumsiness is quite beyond me—their lack of charm and grace.

I do not mean by charm, prettiness, about an appreciation of beauty. Ugliness is beauty, but with a difference, a nobleness that speaks through all the hard crust of convention.

I have heard it said that half the world has nothing to say. Perhaps the other half has, but it is afraid to speak. Banish fear, brace your courage, place your ideal high up with the sun, away from the dirt and squalor and ugliness around you and let that power that makes "the roar of the high-power presses "enter into your work—energy—courage—life—love. Use your wits, use your eyes. Perhaps you use your physical eyes too much and only see the mask. Find eyes within; look for the door into the unknown country.

"High over cap" on a fairy horse ride on your Quest for what we are all seeking—Beauty. Beauty of thought first, beauty of feeling, beauty of form, beauty of color, beauty of sound, appreciation, joy, and the power of showing it to others.

BIBLIOGRAPHY

Kaplan, Stuart R., with Mary K. Greer, Elizabeth Foley O'Connor, and Melinda Boyd Parsons. *Pamela Colman Smith, the Untold Story*. Stamford, CT: U.S. Games Systems, 2018.

Katz, Marcus, and Tali Goodwin. *Secrets of the Waite-Smith Tarot*. Woodbury, MN: Llewellyn, 2015.

ABOUT THE AUTHOR

SCOTT MARTIN began pursuing his fascination with Tarot after retiring as a secondary and college theater arts teacher, director, and mentor in 2009. He holds a BA degree in speech and theater from Indiana University and an MFA degree in directing from Brooklyn College. He has also worked as a professional actor and director.

He combined that love for theater with Tarot in a book he wrote in 2017 titled *Bringing the Tarot to Life: Embody the Cards through Creative Exploration*. In the same year, the book won the Tarosophists Association first prize for Best Mass Market Book of the Year for Innovation and Insight. The book was recently translated into Russian.

In 2021, he wrote *The Silent Doorkeeper: The Alchemical Tarot Shines a Light on Covid-19*, illustrated by Robert M. Place.

Martin has also facilitated a number of Tarot workshops in various venues in New York City. Visit his website at scottmartintarot.com. You can contact him at info@scottmartintarot.com to request a class or workshop.